From Bingley to Borneo

Borneo

Memoirs of a Vice Consul

S. Ian Wall

Order this book online at www.trafford.com
or email orders@trafford.com

Most Trafford titles are also available at major online book retailers.

Printed in Victoria, BC, Canada.

ISBN: 978-1-4269-0311-3 (Soft)
ISBN: 978-1-4269-2292-3 (e-book)

*We at Trafford believe that it is the responsibility of us all, as both individuals
and corporations, to make choices that are environmentally and socially sound.
You, in turn, are supporting this responsible conduct each time you purchase a
Trafford book, or make use of our publishing services. To find out how you are
helping, please visit www.trafford.com/responsiblepublishing.html*

*Our mission is to efficiently provide the world's finest, most comprehensive
book publishing service, enabling every author to experience success.
To find out how to publish your book, your way, and have it available
worldwide, visit us online at www.trafford.com*

Trafford rev. 11/10/2009

Trafford PUBLISHING® www.trafford.com

North America & international
toll-free: 1 888 232 4444 (USA & Canada)
phone: 250 383 6864 ♦ fax: 812 355 4082 ♦ email: info@trafford.com

For my beautiful wife Kelly Meng Ying,
who I love more than ever and forever

Acknowledgements

Thanks go to my daughter Joanne for taking the time from her busy schedule to proof read my book and for her valuable suggestions.

Thanks also to Victor Chai from Borneo Life who provided me with some of the photographs which appear in the book and on the front cover.

Chapter 1

What is it about a cold beer that is just so refreshing on a hot and humid day? As I look out over Ho Hai lakes here in Beijing, it's surface on fire from the sunburnt orange reflection of the setting sun, an involuntary chuckles escapes as I think about the text message I received earlier in the day. Another country on the list!! She'll soon be over taking my 45. I should explain. My daughter Joanne and I have a competition as to who has visited the most number of countries; for years I have been in the lead but slowly and surely she's catching up. 45 countries, probably not as many as John Simpson (the famous BBC news correspondent) but nevertheless a rather respectable total, one which I may have to expand should Joanne get close to overtaking me. She is already snapping at my heels – only 3 or 4 behind me now – and travels a lot with her job.

I order my second glass of beer – the one which you savour. The first doesn't seem to touch the sides but merely quenches that dry thirst. As I'm waiting for the beer to arrive I'm feeling reflective and very content. Lots of experiences – who would have thought that a working class boy from Bingley, West Yorkshire would end up here and what a varied journey.

The brain is a funny thing – I can't for the life of me remember where I left my mobile phone this morning but my memories from years gone by are vivid and crisp.

Having been part of a troublesome group of pupils who questioned the value of being at school and didn't pay attention, I left school, unsurprisingly, at 14 years old with no qualifications whatsoever. Understandably my job prospects were not good. I was almost 17 when I realised that I had just about reached rock bottom in the job market and was on a downward spiral – how much deeper could I go? I was working for British Rail as a lad porter on the railway station in Driffield, East Yorkshire. This involved doing menial tasks such as collecting tickets, sweeping the platform, sorting parcels, and lighting fires in the waiting rooms in winter. It was during one such mind numbing day that I began to wonder what on earth I was doing and where my life was taking me.

Before we go forward, let me set the scene from the very beginning. I had been born in my great grandmother's house in Arthur Street, Bingley, which was a small textile town with a population of around 21,000, in the West Riding of Yorkshire, just before the end of the Second World War. Not that I remember anything about that. It was 1946 by the time my father returned from whatever he had been doing in the war with the Parachute regiment and bought a back to back terraced house in Raven Street – about quarter of a mile from my great grandmother's house. A back to back house is a house which has one door and neighbours on 3 sides. One on the right, one on the left and one family whose living room was at the back of our living room but whose house was actually in the next street There are not many of those kind of houses left now because they were later considered unhealthy places to live.

A couple of years after my father came back and had already resumed his job as a weaving over-looker in Parklands which was one of the many textile mills operating in Bingley at that time, we moved 'up market' to a larger house – a through terraced house - in Heath Street, a short distance away but in the same area. So instead of having just one door to the house with one room down stairs and a small kitchen area at the top of the cellar steps – not big enough to swing a cat around - we had two doors, a back door and a front door (which was hardly ever used) and two rooms downstairs, a living room and a lounge plus quite a large kitchen (compared to the one at the top of the cellar steps we had had previously). There were two bedrooms on the second floor and a bathroom – but no toilet. Like a lot of the houses at that time, the toilet was outside in the back yard next to the coal shed – or coal hole as it was known. We had a chamber pot, or poe as we used to call it, by the side of the beds each night. We also had two attics above the bedrooms which were useful storage spaces initially before being converted into bedrooms at a later stage for my sister and me as we got older and my younger brother was born. There was also two cellars, one underneath the living room and one underneath the lounge. We did not have central heating at that time so we spent most of the time in the living/ dining room because the heat from the kitchen and the fire in the room made it much warmer. We even used to get bathed in there in front of the fire – especially in winter. A large Zinc bath was dragged up from the cellar once a week (whether we needed a bath or not) and filled with hot water from boiling kettles and pans on the stove. I remember that it was always my sister, who is 18 months older than me, who got into the clean bath water first. I always had to go in after her – not that I minded very much - maybe I was just dirtier than she was most of the time – or it could have been that I always peed in the bath – which was probably the real reason why I was last in.

The front room (lounge) was hardly ever used, unless it was a special occasion such as Christmas, because it would have meant having two fires – and coal was expensive, although having said that, my sister and I used to go in there occasionally to play 75rpm gramophone records on an old second-hand wind-up gramophone which Dad bought for us from a junk shop. There were fire places in the two bedrooms upstairs but they were never ever used – again because it would have been too expensive to light them. You could have hung meat in the bedrooms in winter because it was so cold. Each morning in winter you could see your breath, as if your stomach was on fire and the insides of the window panes were covered with thick frost from the condensation which had frozen solid. Certainly not for the faint hearted.

The pantry, which was where all the perishable items were kept, was the area at the top of the cellar steps because it was always cold down there regardless of whether it was summer or winter. Not many people had refrigerators, which were both expensive and not freely available in those days, so fresh milk was kept on the second step from the top and any items which might melt such as lard or margarine were kept on shelves which were fixed to the cellar head wall. The wooden box which my father had made to keep the shoe cleaning material in was kept on the top step of the cellar steps. I always considered it to be my safety box. When my sister and I used to play in the cellar she would often go running up the cellar steps without warning, switch off the light and leave me alone in the dark. I used to be scared stiff and run like crazy up the steps frightened to death that something or someone, a bogeyman, who I was convinced lived down there and came out when it was dark, would grab me from behind. Once I could see the shoe box I knew I had reached safety. I still have the shoe box today – it is worthless to anyone else but it is still holds precious memories for me. When my father died a few years ago, my sister and I were sorting out the contents of his house, deciding which of his belongings we should keep and which we should dispose of, I asked her if she would mind if I had the shoe box and told her the reason why. She smiled and said 'Sorry – I didn't realise – of course you can have it'.

My Dad was still working as a weaving overlooker by this time and was even working night shifts in the mill to try to increase his pay packet from GBP10 per week to GBP20 per week. This extra amount was because they got more pay for working the longer night shifts. My Mother was also working for a short time after my sister and I started school until my brother was born in 1955. She worked at the factory at the bottom of our street which made spring clips, but I don't think she liked it very much so her pregnancy gave her the opportunity to leave.

Growing up at that time there was not so much to do indoors - my dad bought a black and white television (9 inch screen) in 1953 (just in time for the Queen's coronation – when it seemed that every man and his dog came around to watch). Television was in its infancy then and the broadcasts did not start until late afternoon (children's hour) and closed down quite early in the evenings, around 9 or 10pm after the National Anthem. Most of the time, especially during the day, we had to make our own pleasure. We used to go on family outings at the weekends – when I say outings it was either going to the local cricket ground to watch cricket or else going for really long walks either over Ilkley moor or along the Leeds/Liverpool canal bank to various parks and woods, or to visit my Dad's parents and his many brothers and sisters who were scattered in little villages around Bingley. We also had an annual holiday each summer when the mill closed. Sometimes it was for a week and if we were lucky sometimes two. We didn't generally go very far – it was mostly seaside resorts on either the Lancashire or Yorkshire coasts, although one time we did venture down south to Hasting.

Sunday was probably the best day of the week in lots of ways. We used to get up early so that my sister and I could go to the local swimming baths with our Dad. It opened at 8am and we were always one of the first families in the queue. We would swim and play for about 45 minutes and then go home again to a large cooked breakfast of bacon, eggs, sausage, fried tomatoes and fried bread, which Mum always had waiting for us. We were like hungry wolves after swimming. The fried breakfast was a real treat, because for the rest of the week it was usually a sandwich with either apple, banana or thin slices of fried potato in the middle. After breakfast we had to put on our Sunday best clothes and it was off to the Methodist chapel for 10 o'clock Sunday School - which was fine whilst I was young but I started to have my doubts about the chapel and Christianity in general when I got older and stopped going altogether. Lunch (or Dinner as we used to call it) on Sunday was also a meal we all looked forward to – we generally had really big pieces of Yorkshire pudding as our starter, served on its own with gravy first – the traditional way – followed by the second course, roast beef, mashed potatoes and vegetables with more lovely thick gravy. Yorkshire pudding, is made from a sort of pancake mixture of plain flour, eggs, milk, and then cooked in the oven for about 20 minutes until it rises. It was really used as a kind of filler before the main course because meat was expensive and the joints of meat we could afford were very small. The only trouble with my Mum's cooking was that she belonged to the old school of cooks as far as vegetables were concerned, she thought that you had to put the Brussels sprouts on to boil in October ready for Christmas Day. Desert varied each week but I used to love the small dried fruit based sponge puddings called Goblin puddings – a bit like a miniature Christmas pudding - with thick custard. We also had our weekly treat - a bottle of Tizer and a bottle of Dandelion & Burdock with our lunch (dinner). Dandelion & Burdock is a very dark looking carbonated drink which looks very much like a beer – a bit like sarsaparilla. I always imagined I was grown up drinking stout when I drank this. Depending on the season, in the afternoons we generally went for a long walk or went to play cricket or football in a park.

During the week, all year round, I used to spend lots of time outdoors – even in winter. In winter we played football and touch rugby and in summer it was cricket. All the games were played in the school yard close to our house. Selecting who would play on what team, especially when it came to football, was quite brutal in a way. The two best players – usually the two oldest boys - were nominated as captains of each side and they then stood in front of the rest of us and took it in turns to select who they wanted to play on their teams. When it was football, I and another boy (Donald) were almost always the last to be selected, maybe because we were both pretty clumsy on our feet and did not have very good football skills. Rugby and Cricket, where the ball is in the hand – was a different ball game and I was always one of the first to be selected.

When not playing these games I was generally just getting up to mischief with all the other boys of my age – climbing trees and walls, breaking street gas lamps with our catapults, stealing fruit from orchards and all that kind of stuff. Friendships were made outside, regardless of the weather. We rarely visited each others homes, apart from calling to ask if a friend was 'coming out to play'. We all enjoyed being outside because most of the houses which we lived in were quite small and television was still in its infancy.

During the long school summer holiday, just after my younger brother was born and shortly before I started Grammar school, my friend Donald and I were wandering around the town one day, in search of something to do when we came across quite a large stagnant pond with a small island in the middle of it, in the grounds of a large old house. The pond itself, known locally as Hanson's pond, was surrounded by trees and bushes. Whilst we were looking around we discovered a couple of oil drums quite near the pond. Being fans of Richmal Compton's William books and Enid Blyton's Secret Seven books, we decided that we would have our own little adventure and build a raft. We hid the oil drums under some bushes so no one else would find them and then started to try and find the wood to make the rest of the raft. There was nothing really useful lying around so we decided to go to our homes to see if we could find anything suitable there. He searched in his house and I looked around in my great grandmother's cellar because her house was close to where my friend Donald lived. I found an old wooden hearth fender which used to sit in front of the coal fire and Donald found some other pieces of wood in his cellar. I also 'borrowed' a machete looking axe from my great grandmother's cellar and off we went back to the pond again, loaded up with wood to build the raft – Kontiki here we come. We spent a couple of days building it, using saplings which we had chopped off the trees near the pond and thin pieces of bark to fasten it all together – real Robinson Crusoe stuff - until finally it was ready. The oil drums were lowered into the water and the framework we had built was placed on top. The time had come to decide which one of us was going to take her on her maiden voyage. I think we drew straws, (or in this case pieces of twigs) and I got the short one so I lost. Donald gingerly crept onboard, grinning all over his face and crouched in the centre of the raft and I gave him a gentle push off. He started punting his way with a long stick across the pond to the other side, where we were had agreed we would change places so that I could have a turn. He was really enjoying himself and I was quite envious that I was not on the raft, until half way across the pond, the stick he was using to propel the raft got stuck in the mud at the bottom of the pond. Instead of waiting for me to throw him another stick from the side, he decided to try free the stick he had been using by pulling it out of the mud himself. Unfortunately in order to do this he had to get closer to the edge of the raft. As soon as he moved from the central position, the raft was no longer balanced and as it overturned the oil drums shot into the air – like submarine depth charges being fired from a warship. It looked so funny, especially as he was swimming back to the side of the pond. I just couldn't stop laughing – there he was breast stroking it back to the side and all I could see was his head and his round national health spectacles – later made fashionable by John Lennon. All he could say, as he was spitting out pond water from his mouth, was 'you wouldn't be laughing if you were here'. It was even funnier once he got out of the water because his thick woollen jumper and thick short pants had acted like sponges and he was dripping water all over the place. He had also lost one of his wellington boots whilst swimming to the side so when he started running home all I could see on the pavement as I followed him was one wet sock mark every few metres – all in a straight line. The sole of his remaining wellington boot had dried but his sock hadn't – it was like following a one legged man or a kangaroo who was hopping. I could hardly keep up with him for laughing.

As you will have gathered, I was not the best of pupils once I got to Grammar School – I started out enthusiastically enough but gradually seemed to lose interest in the lessons, especially French and Maths. I was always near the bottom of the class – never quite bottom but near enough to realise that I was not destined for University. The only thing I was any good at was sport. Boys at that school played Rugby in the winter and Cricket in the summer and I was reasonably good at both games – especially Rugby. In later life, I regretted that we had not been allowed to play tennis because as I found out whilst in Malaysia it is a very good game and I used to play on the High Commission tennis court 3 or 4 times per week. Unfortunately at school it was only played by girls so any boy who even thought for a moment about wanting to play tennis was considered to be a bit effeminate.

Rock & Roll was just becoming popular in the UK in 1955 and I was a big Elvis fan. In order to have some money to buy some of his records I decided to get a paper round – delivering newspapers to houses in certain parts of town. I had a morning round and an evening round. The morning round took me about an hour and a half – starting at about 6.30am and finishing about 8am just in time to have some breakfast and to get changed for school. The evening paper round was much shorter – only about 40 minutes but the wages I earned from the two paper rounds was enough to buy a record every so often and also to buy some books and cigarettes. Most of the boys I knew seemed to start smoking at about 11 or 12 years old at that time. Thank goodness I stopped years later.

One day, my Dad came home from the Mill earlier than expected, with his right index finger all bandaged up. He had just come from the hospital. It seemed that whilst he was repairing one of the weaving looms, his apprentice had accidentally switched the power on and the loom burst into life slicing off the end of my Dad's right index finger. He had taken the tip of his the finger with him to the hospital but they had not been able to reattach it. He was off work for a few days until the swelling and the stiffness eased off and eventually received some compensation from the company for the loss of his finger end. I am not sure how much he got, he never did say, but it wasn't long afterwards that he announced that he was going to sell our house (which was worth about GBP400 at that time (now GBP135,000) and buy a Fish & Chip shop in Leeds. I was beside myself, racked with worry. "What would I do in such a big city?" I wouldn't know anyone, all of my friends were in Bingley, but there was nothing I could do about it. The decision had been made. Dad spent a couple of weeks learning about fish frying at our local Fish & Chip shop at the top of our street and shortly afterwards we moved to Armley in Leeds – up Tong Road, not so far from the jail.

Initially my sister and I used to commute by bus and train from Leeds to Bingley each day to attend school but within a few weeks the local Education authority, who were paying our fares, decided because my sister was studying for her O levels (examinations taken by pupils at the age of 16 years old which determined whether or not they were clever enough to go on to study for a further two years and take the A level examinations in order to go to University), that her studies should not be disrupted by moving to another school. She was going to be allowed to continue studying in Bingley, but because I had not yet started my O level studies I should find a place at a school in Leeds.

An interview was subsequently arranged for me to see the Headmaster of Leeds Grammar School – one of the best Grammar schools in Yorkshire if not the whole of UK. At that time a two tier education system existed in the UK. An examination was taken by students when they were 11 years old which determined whether they went to a Grammar School or a Secondary Modern School. Grammar schools were supposed to be for the brighter pupils who appeared to have the potential to eventually go to University. My Dad and I went along at the appointed time. I had been specially groomed before we left home and I was looking very studious – all scrubbed up and hair tidily combed wearing my Bingley Grammar School uniform, holding my school cap. During the course of the interview the headmaster asked me what I wanted to do. I replied that I wanted to leave school at 15 and find a job. Not exactly what the headmaster had expected to hear I don't think. The interview was concluded very shortly after that and we were ushered out. Needless to say I was not accepted. Once we got outside my Dad was livid, and I think would have clipped me around the ears if we hadn't have been in the centre of a busy city. I had blown it and ended up going to Armley Park Secondary Modern School (which was really preparing its students for an existence as blue collar workers by providing them with a basic education). But at least they had an O level stream so I was given a place in that particular class. I didn't do much better there than I had at Bingley Grammar – I liked Geography very much and even surprised myself by coming second in the class in this subject, but there were other subjects where I was second from the bottom. I suppose if I had taken the trouble to revise before examinations I might have done better.

After about a year of living in Leeds my Mother and Father decided that they had had enough of the place and bought another Fish

& Chip shop in Driffield, a little market town in the East Riding of Yorkshire – not too far from the seaside town of Bridlington. We had been to Bridlington on holidays when I was younger and it had been good fun. So we said goodbye to Leeds and I left school before my 15th birthday - never to return.

On the day of the move my Dad went with the removal men in the removal van and my Mother, Sister, younger brother and I travelled the 60 or so miles by bus. As we were walking up the main street in Driffield from the bus stop to where our shop was – I began to wonder what an earth we had let ourselves in for. There was a market place and a pub called the Black Swan – it reminded me of the comedy farces I had seen on television about village life – the market place and the Black Swan pub where all the locals went for a drink nicknamed the mucky duck. Driffield (which boasts to be the Capital of the Wolds) had a population at that time of 8,000 people. Apart from 21 other pubs besides the Black Swan and 2 cinemas – there didn't seem a lot to do there – and there wasn't – so most evenings during the week, or at least part of each evening would be spent in the youth club and the pub – I am not sure how I managed to get served in a pub at 15 but it never seemed to be a problem maybe because all of my new found friends were all 18 or 19 years old.

I had been hoping to find a job as a motor mechanic but there were no positions available for apprentice motor mechanics in any of the garages in the town. I tried my hand at various jobs before descending slowly but surely to the bottom of the pond. I worked as a labourer on a farm for a few weeks during harvest time, shortly after we arrived in Driffield, but that kind of job did not really suit me, being from a textile town in the West Riding of Yorkshire. I even had difficulty understanding the East Riding country yokel accents and I suspect they had a problem with mine. I worked in an optical factory in town cutting out NHS spectacle frames on a machine and later got a job as an apprentice blacksmith (or to give it its posh title – an apprentice agricultural engineer) on a large farming estate. I had imagined that I would be shoeing horses, repairing tractors and combined harvesters etc but I was really only a labourer – humping large metal girders, as well as oxygen and acetylene bottles – and sweeping the floor. Something needed to be done to get me back on the right track – and quickly - because I didn't fancy the thought of sweeping railway platforms or factory floors for the rest of my life – even though after so much practice I was becoming quite an expert with a brush.

Chapter 2

I decided one day, after seeing a film about American sailors at the local cinema, that the Navy was a good idea and would get me out of the rut I was in. Maybe I could learn a trade which would be useful in my later life. The sailors in the film seemed to have a good time, get well paid – more than my GBP2. 3s. 4d old pence per week - and they also had the opportunity to visit lots of different countries and cities all over the world. It seemed a brilliant idea and the ideal solution to my problems. I informed my parents what I planned to do and headed off to the Royal Navy recruitment office in Hull – much to my Mother's dismay. After various aptitude tests and medical examinations in Newcastle I was accepted by the Royal Navy as a Junior Radio Operator. Just after my 17th birthday, in July 1962, I took the overnight train down to Plymouth where I did my basic training for 6 weeks in the Naval shorebase HMS Raleigh. Once the square bashing (marching and physical training) was over it was off to Portsmouth to start my Communications training at the Navy Communication School, HMS Mercury in Petersfield.

The Communications training was about a year altogether, learning the Morse code, semaphore, visual signalling, typing, and various kinds of voice, radio and fleetwork procedures before eventually I was drafted to my first ship – HMS Plover. She was a small minelayer (which I was told when I arrived would roll on wet grass because of its flat bottom and shallow draft – and it did

- luckily I was not prone to seasickness). It was a small ship and was very cramped. No one on the lower deck had a proper bunk so there were people sleeping all over the place, on tables, under tables – just about everywhere. I ended up sleeping in a hammock on the mining deck just outside the engine room hatch – with mines below my hammock during exercises.

I was drafted to a number of ships during my naval career, most of them the sea going variety – not shore bases, or as we sailors called them, concrete frigates. I spent some time in the Far East on HMS Diana (Daring Class Destroyer) and HMS Cambrian (CA Class Destroyer), and around the UK waters on HMS Lofoten (a war time tank landing craft which had been converted into a Helicopter support ship), before eventually joining the guided missile destroyer HMS Hampshire which was on world wide service. I was on that ship for 3 years which felt like a lifetime. The only good thing about it was that we visited quite a lot of countries – especially around the Mediterranean and South America. One of my shipmates, Dixie Dean from Northern Ireland, used to complain that he had got engaged to his girlfriend whilst he was on the Hampshire, he had got married on the Hampshire and his wife had given birth to twins and he was still on the bloody Hampshire. She eventually decommissioned and I was drafted to HMS Mauritius – which was a Royal Naval Communications shore base on the Island of Mauritius in the Indian Ocean for 2 years. What a wonderful place to end my ten years in the Navy – a concrete frigate at last. What a pleasure, a paradise island surrounded by warm turquoise coloured sea water, and white sands. I was married by then and my wife was expecting our first baby, so it was an ideal place to end my naval career. My daughter was 6 weeks old by the time I first saw her when the British Airways stewardess handed her over to me at Plaisance Airport, whilst my wife was completing her immigration process, it was love at first sight. I used to say to her that she had to be born in Yorkshire just in case she had been a boy, so that he could play cricket for Yorkshire. At that time no one could play cricket for Yorkshire unless they had been born in the county of Yorkshire. It was quite a few years later before the decision was taken to allow 'foreign' players (even from Lancashire) into the team. The two years spent in Mauritius were wonderful, I used to work shifts (2 days on and 2 days off) so had plenty of time off to enjoy the weather and the beautiful beaches with my family. My earlier love of Rugby hadn't left me and I played lots of rugby whilst I was in Mauritius, sometimes 2 or 3 games a week and was eventually made captain of the national rugby team – an International at last. My daughter used to come and watch me play and used to run on to the pitch at half time for a hug. She watched so much rugby when she was young that she was convinced that in order to kick a ball whether it was a football or tennis ball, it was first necessary to dig a little hole in the ground with her heel, place the ball in the hole and then kick it. Very amusing but it probably came very natural to her after watching so much rugby.

One of my jobs in the Communications Centre (Comcen) of HMS Mauritius was to send telegrams for the British High Commission in Port Louis, the capital city of Mauritius, to the Foreign & Commonwealth Office (FCO) in London because they had no direct secure communications links. The telegrams were delivered to the Comcen every couple of days by one of the diplomats from the High Commission. As the time for my discharge grew nearer I began to wonder what I should do when I left the Navy. I thought briefly about staying on and completing the full 22 years so that I would be able to retire with a pension but the thought of living in such cramped conditions on a warship again after living in an apartment with all the home comforts and a maid did not appeal. Besides which it was only delaying the inevitable – I would have to leave the Navy when I was 40 so leaving at 27 seemed a much better age to be entering the job market.

The Foreign Office sounded like a good job – lots of overseas travel which is what I had grown used to – maybe it was worth a try. I asked the guy who brought the telegrams if he could give me the address of the Diplomatic Wireless Service (DWS) so that I could write to them to ask about job opportunities. I was initially turned down by DWS who said they were not recruiting at that time but a couple of weeks later they wrote to me with the address of another government organisation and suggested that I might like to apply to them for a job.– which I did. I was lucky to get in. I think the main reason I was accepted was because the guy who interviewed me over a period of 6 months, throughout the long vetting process, was a fanatical Welsh Rugby supporter. Each time we met all we did was talk about Rugby – it was at the time when the Welsh Rugby team were almost unbeatable. I am convinced, to this day, that it was the Rugby which got me the job. After 3 years with the Government Communications Bureau, which was based in Century House, just south of the river Thames, in London, I was eventually successful in transferring to the Diplomatic Wireless Service,

It was quite funny really about 25 years later when I went down to Pretoria in South Africa on a business trip from Malawi, (where I had been posted as Management Officer/Consul), to buy some furniture and other items for the British High Commission in Lilongwe, I met the guy in the British Embassy in Pretoria who had given me the address of DWS. I recognised his face and knew that I had met him somewhere but couldn't for the life of me think where. It dawned on me in the middle of the night, as it often does when you go to bed with a problem which you can't immediately solve – it was Mauritius. I asked him the next day if he had been in Mauritius in 1971 and he had. So I told him that he was the man who had given me the address to write to join DWS. He surprised me by saying 'I'm so sorry', but I assured him that I had enjoyed every minute of it. Such a small world.

I had various postings overseas with the Diplomatic Wireless Service including Islamabad (Pakistan), Darwin (Australia), Tehran (Iran), Sana'a (Yemen), Beijing (China), Moscow (USSR - where I was expelled as a spy), and Pretoria (South Africa). It was interesting work but I realised after a few years that the writing was on the wall for my particular profession and that technology was advancing so quickly that we would soon be obsolete – dinosaurs – out of a job. I therefore decided that the only way to stay in the Foreign Office was to get some educational qualifications so that I could join the mainstream FCO. At the age of 34 I did my O and A levels whilst on a posting with DWS to Darwin in Australia and eventually completed my six year Bachelor of Arts degree (distance learning) with the Open University whilst on my final posting with DWS in Pretoria. Eventually after attending an interview board in the FCO I was allowed to transfer to the FCO and spent a couple of years in London working in the Consular Department before being told in 1991 that I was being posted to the British High Commission in Kuala Lumpur (Malaysia) as Vice Consul. I had visited KL before when HMS Cambrian had stopped off in Singapore and was very much looking forward to returning there.

Chapter 3

Within a matter of weeks of arriving in Kuala Lumpur, after I had settled into the job and our accommodation, which was situated in the High Commission grounds at the back; the Consul, John Greengrass, informed me that it was time to make a Consular trip to East Malaysia (Sarawak – the land of the hornbills and Sabah – the land below the winds) on the island of Borneo. He had been there himself a couple of times whilst he was Vice Consul but now that he had been promoted to Consul he had no desire to fly off to visit different parts of Malaysia for days on end leaving his family behind – he would stay in KL and look after the shop. There was one exception to this rule however, and that was the Consular trips to Penang. He would be making all the Consular trips to Penang because he could drive there and take his family with him so that they could spend the day on the beach whilst he was working. All the rest of the Consular trips – all over Malaysia, both peninsular and East Malaysia, were mine - which suited me fine.

I was delighted to be taking off on another adventure so soon after arriving. I had been off Borneo on HMS Cambrian, during the Indonesian confrontation in 1965/66 but never been ashore there so the thought of actually setting foot on Borneo and visiting new places and meeting new people was a very exciting prospect. Consular trips can best be likened to a British Member of Parliament's constituency surgeries because members of the public would make appointments and come along with their Immigration/Nationality queries and I was there to provide the answers to their questions. The first step was to make a courtesy telephone call to the Consular wardens (sort of Honorary Consuls who acted on the High Commission's behalf – generally British ex-patriots) in the cities to be visited to ask whether the dates of my proposed trip would be convenient for them. The second step was to place an advertisement in the Borneo Post – which is circulated throughout East Malaysia, to let members of the public know where and on what dates and in what cities I would be available for consultations. The cities to be visited on this particular trip were Kuching and Miri in Sarawak and Kota Kinabalu in Sabah. The Consular wardens in Kuching and Kota Kinabalu were both Bank Managers. In Kuching the warden was the Manager of Standard Chartered Bank and in Kota Kinabalu the warden was the Manager of the Hong Kong Shanghai Bank. In Miri the warden was one of the Managers at the Petronas Oil refinery complex. I was kindly offered an office in the Standard Chartered Bank in Kuching and would be using an office in the British Council in Kota Kinabalu. In Miri the clinics were to be held in one of the offices in the Petronas oil refinery complex at Lutong a short drive outside of town. The third and final step was to book hotel accommodation in each city. In Kuching it was to be the Holiday Inn, in Miri the Park Hotel (the best hotel in town so I was told) and in Kota Kinabalu the Hyatt hotel.

The day of departure soon came around and I headed off to the airport full of excitement and anticipation carrying my suitcase and a large brief case full of various kinds of Immigration and passport application forms as well as a couple of receipt books and rubber stamps. The flight from KL to Kuching was about an hour and a half and arrived at about 6 o'clock in the evening. On the flight, I noticed that there were quite a few ex-pat businessmen who were also going to Kuching. I realised, once we arrived, that they must have been regular commuters between KL and

Kuching because I had checked my suitcase into the hold of the aircraft and they all had fold up suit bags which they had kept with them as hand luggage. The penny dropped once I reached the hotel. They must have all arrived at the hotel and checked into their rooms whilst I was still waiting for my suitcase to be off loaded from the aircraft. By the time I arrived at the Holiday Inn hotel, (which is beautifully situated at the side of the Sarawak River), checked in and unpacked my suitcase and found my way down to the Rajang Bar, they were all on their second or third drinks grinning at me as I walked in. I made a mental note to buy a folding suit bag as soon as the trip was over.

After a very enjoyable evening in the Rajang Bar making new friends – who seemed to frequent the place every night – for the Happy Hour at least, I was awake early next morning and had breakfast in the hotel restaurant – fried bee hoon (thin fried noodles with cabbage, mushrooms, diced red and green chillies and prawns). What a wonderful way to start the day. I was at the Bank, just across the road from the hotel by 9am - ready for my first Consular Clinic.

The Manager of the Standard Chartered Bank was a very friendly Yorkshireman called John who made me feel very welcome and showed me to the office which I would be occupying for the next 2 days. Coffee was delivered to the office by one of his staff almost before I had unpacked all the forms. The first client, a middle aged lady, arrived shortly afterwards. A complex nationality case – something I was dreading. What a way to start my first Consular trip – nothing like being thrown in at the deep end. Some nationality applications can be like a minefield – especially this one which involved lots and lots of what seemed to be very ancient documents. My mind went blank and I was totally confused by them all so decided in the end that the best course of action (and to save face) was to accept all of her documents so that I could take them all back to KL and look at the case in more detail – and also to seek some guidance from the Consul. My boss laughingly told me later that this lady always makes an application to see the visiting Consular staff – especially, a new one who she hasn't seen before – in the hope that someone, sometime will take pity on her and tell her she is eligible for British Citizenship and issue her and her family with British passports. He wasn't in the least bit surprised that she had been my first client; she had been his first client each time he had been over there. I wonder if she is still trying and is still the first in the queue each time someone from the High Commission goes over to Kuching. The rest of the appointments, thankfully, were pretty much straightforward, mainly proud parents with their student off-springs who wanted to further their studies in the UK. I accepted all of their documents with the assurance that their passports and their supporting documents would be posted back to them once their student visas had been issued. After 2 days my briefcase was beginning to fill up. Fortunately I managed to unload a number of blank visa and passport applications on to the Bank Manager so that he could hand them out to prospective applicants for them to complete and hand in to me the next time I was in town. It was a relief to be able to offload a pile of forms so my brief case was not overfull. Next stop Miri about an hours flight up country.

Miri at that time was a bit like a Wild West Town. Lots of oil workers used to come down to Miri – and probably still do - from the state of Brunei. Brunei is a small, oil rich, mainly Muslim country situated between Sarawak and Sabah where there is no alcohol. It is only about half an hours drive away from Miri so lots of the foreign oil workers used to drive over the border to have a boozy night out on the town and visit the bars and nightclubs. I found the Park Hotel eventually, which after the comfort of the Holiday Inn in Kuching was a bit of a letdown. It was a dirty, dingy little hotel which was not quite what I had expected. If this is the best hotel in town – I certainly didn't want to see the worst. I had a room at the back of the hotel which I assumed would be quiet because it was away from the main road. Little did I know that directly beneath my room, was the entrance to the nightclub and there was also a bus terminus situated at the back of the hotel. After unpacking my clothes and freshening up I decided to have a walk around the town to see what it was like. It didn't take very long. I stopped off in a bar for a couple of drinks on the way back to the hotel and had dinner in a restaurant close by. Feeling pretty shattered after my busy 2 days and nights in Kuching I decided to have an early night and was in bed by about 9pm. Well it wasn't long after that before the music from the Nightclub started blasting out on full volume. I had just put my book down and was falling asleep when the silence was shattered – I was almost horizontal a foot above the mattress with the shock. The decibels were blasting out all night long until about 4.30am. I was shattered and feeling pretty grumpy by that time after being kept awake all night long. Just as I was falling asleep I was awakened again by the sound of buses tooting their horns as they were leaving the bus terminus to set off on their routes to collect the early morning workers. What a night – I hadn't slept a wink and felt exhausted. Thank goodness I was only in the Park Hotel for one night. It was my first and only stay in that hotel in all the years I visited East Malaysia.

After a shave and shower and a small breakfast – the food in the hotel was as bad as the room - I took a taxi out to the Lutong, on the outskirts of town, which is where the Petronas complex is located, to get myself ready for the next Consular clinic. The ride out there along a nice new road was quite pleasant. There were lots of trees and jungle on one side of the road and some very nice houses leading down to the sea, where a lot of the Petronas senior officials lived, on the other side. The sun was shining and the heat was beginning to build up and it felt good to be alive and in East Malaysia.

It was not a particularly busy day – most of the applications were from British Oil-workers who wanted to either renew their British passports or apply for British passports for their new born off-springs. One of them – a Liverpudlian called Bill Fowler came along with his Malaysian wife Pauline and their young son to apply for a British Passport for him. Being from the North of England myself we struck up a good friendship and remained friends for all the time I was in Malaysia. Sadly Bill died some years ago but I still keep in touch with his wife Pauline and her son – who is now almost 18 years old and going to University and also has a younger brother of 14.

My last client of the day had not come to see me about any passport or immigration issue – it was something else entirely. She was a very pretty young lady who had come to see me to ask if I could help her to find her British boyfriend. She told me that they had been going out together for quite a few months but he had suddenly left Miri when he found out she was pregnant. I felt sorry for her but wasn't able to help her other than suggest that she speak to someone in the Human Resources department at Petronas to ask them if they knew where he had gone. I bade farewell to Miri late in the afternoon and headed back to the airport for the flight to Kota Kinabalu – feeling shattered after a sleepless night but very satisfied with the day's business. My briefcase was getting fuller all the time.

I arrived in Kota Kinabalu quite late in the evening and was surprised how dreary the area around the Hyatt hotel seemed to be compared to the area around the Holiday Inn in Kuching. There were streets and streets of oblong blocks of concrete 4 storey apartments running parallel to each other with shops and restaurants on the ground floor – something like what you would have seen in Russia or China at that time. I guessed they must have been built in a hurry to replace the buildings which had been bombed by the Japanese during the Second World War. The place seemed filthy because there was lots of rubbish lying around in the streets and even more it seemed in the large open monsoon drains which ran parallel with the pavement. The hotel itself was lovely though, especially after my night in the Park Hotel in Miri. It was 5 star and very comfortable. From my room I had a good view over the South China Sea and there were no nightclubs or bus depots that I could see or hear! I unpacked and decided to do a quick recce to try and find out where the British Council offices were so that I would not get lost next morning. Luckily they were not too far away – because walking in a suit, carrying a brief case in the hot humid climate of Malaysia, even early in the morning, quickly works a sweat up, and I didn't want to arrive at their offices looking like a drowned rat.

After a good nights sleep and hearty breakfast I arrived at the British Council Offices next morning and set up shop in one of their spare offices. I wasn't late but by the time I arrived there were a few eager students already waiting for me. Luckily for them the waiting area was in the library part of the British Council so they had lots of books, newspapers and magazines to keep them occupied. Before I started work I telephoned the Hong Kong Shanghai Bank to let the warden know that I was in town and he very kindly invited me to have dinner with him that night. The two days went off without any hitches and I collected a large number of student visa applications from would be scholars wanting to study in the UK. No difficult cases and my briefcase was just about bursting, with about 100 passports and thousands of Malaysian Ringgit.

Dinner with the warden was quite a grand affair. He had invited me to have dinner with him and his wife at the Kota Kinabalu Yacht club where all the well heeled businessmen in Kota Kinabalu and their wives used to meet to have a drink and catch up on the local gossip. The food was excellent and so was the Johnny Walker Black label, at least that is what I assumed, judging by the large quantities of it which the warden drank that night. He was a jovial, entertaining and very amusing character and the evening was an absolute pleasure. It became a bit of a ritual after that – each time I went over to Kota Kinabalu we used to end up in the Yacht club for drinks and dinner. When I got back to the hotel – in a happy frame of mind - I decided to have a night cap in the lobby bar before going to bed. I was intrigued by the number of beautiful young girls wearing bright yellow jackets and tight black trousers, almost like tights, who were getting into the lifts to go to various guests rooms – I thought they looked like bees - very busy bees. I found out on another trip that they were the massage girls – who were very obliging – so I am told…..

Chapter 4

Well that was my first Consular trip out of the way and I felt it had been very successful – both from a business point of view and socially. So it was back to Kuala Lumpur to do the more mundane tasks of conducting Entry Clearance interviews on a daily basis – but they turned out to be less mundane that I had expected.

It wasn't long before I had my first strange visa applicants – made even more suspicious because as Malaysian citizens they did not require a visas to visit the UK. They were a young Chinese couple – boyfriend and girlfriend so they said – who wanted to spend a couple of weeks on holiday in the UK.

I interviewed the young man first in the interview room, which had a glass partition between me and the clients with a hole at the bottom where documents could be passed between. First of all I asked him why he was applying for a visa when it was not necessary for him to have one to visit the UK. He told me that he would feel happier and safer with a visa because he had heard of people having problems with the Immigration Officers when they arrived at London Heathrow airport. I started the interview and went through the usual questions of asking him what he did for a living, how long he had been doing it for, what his salary was, what he would be doing when he arrived in the UK, how long he planned to stay there and where he would be staying. He looked a bit of a shifty character and seemed totally unsure about what he would be doing in the UK – besides which he could not name any of the sights he wanted to see and was even unsure where he would stay. I asked him how much money he would be taking and he produced GBP5,000 in notes. I wasn't convinced about him so I asked him to wait outside and to send his girlfriend into the interview room. She came in, looking absolutely stunning, and I asked her similar questions to what I had asked her boyfriend. When I asked her what she would be doing in the UK and how long she planned to stay – she also had no idea. She produced a large wad of notes – identical to the one her boyfriend had shown me - GBP5,000 again. It looked pretty suspicious so I called Siu Pi, one of the Visa Assistants, who worked in the General office to ask the young Chinese man to show her his money at the visa section counter. I was not surprised when Siu Pi called me back to say that he couldn't - because he had given it to his girlfriend so that she could show it to me. I decided then that they were definitely up to no good and started to tell the young lady that I was going to refuse her application. As soon as I had finished telling her why I was going to refuse her she started to unbutton her blouse, which was concealing a beautiful pair of breasts and said "there must be something I can do which will change your mind". I couldn't believe what she was doing – I was beside myself – my heart was pounding and all I could think of saying was – get out – go back into the waiting room and I will issue your notice of refusal from the general office counter. I suppose by doing this she had confirmed my suspicions of what the pair of them were likely to be getting up to if they had got their visas to travel to the UK. But maybe, just maybe, I should have waited a little bit longer to see how far she was prepared to go – at the other side of the glass - to help me change my mind........

One of my regular tasks was to read the daily newspaper each day to see if there were any articles in there related to British Citizens who were in distress. It didn't happen very often but on one particular occasion I found an article in it about a Scot who had been removed from an aircraft which had arrived at Kuala Lumpur International Airport from Australia for being drunk and disorderly. The article described him as being Scottish and also 2.7 metres tall. I presumed it was a misprint until I read that he had put 6 airport security staff in hospital and one of them was in Intensive care. Maybe it wasn't a misprint after all. The article indicated which Police Station he was being detained at, pending trial, so I phoned the police station and spoke to the Officer in Charge and asked if I could go along there to visit his prisoner. He readily agreed and I went down to the police station in the afternoon after I had finished my morning entry clearance interviews. Upon arrival at the Police Station I was taken to meet the Officer in Charge in his office and we had a short chat about what had happened and he told me that all the airport security officers had just about recovered from their ordeals. He suggested that his prisoner (my client) be brought up to his office so that I could meet him. I must admit that I was not too sure about the wisdom of this idea and reminded him that this man had put 6 people in hospital and perhaps it was better if we visited him whilst he was behind bars in his cell. He was having none of this (maybe because he didn't want me to see the state of the police cells) and instructed one of his officers to go and bring the prisoner up to his office. Well I sat there feeling a certain amount of trepidation – I am 1.9 metres tall but the thought of someone who is 2.7 metres tall, with a history of violence made me feel a little bit uncomfortable. A short time later there was a knock on the door and in walked a police officer followed by an absolute giant of a man. He was as tall as the newspaper article had stated and weighed about 350 pounds. To my surprise when I stood up to introduce myself and shake his hand, my rather large hand completely disappeared inside his great paw as I was gazing up at him – it was like shaking hands with a shovel. Thankfully he was full of remorse and very sorry for what had happened. He told me that he was on his way back to the UK having just divorced his wife in Australia. He had been drowning his sorrows with whisky all the way from Sydney to Kuala Lumpur and it was whilst the plane was refuelling and being cleaned ready to receive the joining passengers that the trouble started. He had demanded more whisky and was told politely that he could not have any more drinks until the plane took off again. Upon hearing this he went berserk and started shouting for more whisky which was why the airport security staff was called to remove him from the flight. He took offence at this and laid into all of them before finally being subdued by superior numbers.

He was tried a few days later and sentenced to 3 months in Pudu prison which is in the centre of Kuala Lumpur. The prison, which was constructed between 1891 and 1895, is surrounded by a large wall on which the inmates used 2000 litres of paint over a 12 month period to paint murals all the way around the outside. It closed in November 1996 and has now become a tourist attraction.

I used to visit him every few weeks to make sure that he was being looked after properly and not being subjected to any worse treatment than the local inmates. I also used to take him some toiletries, biscuits and some reading material. He was fine at first but it wasn't long before, on one of my visits, that he started complaining about being locked up and the way that other prisoners were treating him. He said they were all making fun of him and calling him weird. I had to smile and reminded him of how tall he was and that he was weird compared to the rest of the inmates – he was twice their size in height and weight so it was no wonder they thought he was strange. I felt pretty safe doing this especially as he was handcuffed. He told me he was itching to have a night out in Kuala Lumpur because his fellow inmates had told him how good it was. Fortunately he was taken straight to the airport from the prison once he had completed his sentence

– which was probably as well – he may have hit the whisky again and created another Consular problem for me.

On the same day that I was going to the police station to see the giant, I had received a phone call from a British National who was having a few problems on the Thai/ Malaysian border. It seems that he had been detained on the Malaysian side when he crossed over from Thailand – something to do with his passport. I explained that I would not be able to get up to see him until the following day because I was busy with a Consular case in Kuala Lumpur. He seemed pretty relaxed about this and responded by telling me that 'in the meantime he would keep a stiff upper lip'. It sounded very droll and I wondered what kind of person he was – his voice didn't sound very old on the telephone but his terminology was a bit 'old world'.

I took a flight up to Penang the following morning and then hired a car to drive up to the Immigration post on the border with Thailand. As I walked in, I saw a young man, wearing a jungle green coloured safari suit with shorts, jungle green socks and brown boots. He was standing there leaning on, of all things, a black rolled umbrella!! I immediately thought – this is my man. When I walked up to him and introduced myself, he was actually surprised that I had been able to identify him so easily. It wasn't difficult – he was the only one white person in the building and the only one person in the whole place dressed like that. Keeping up appearances it seemed as well as a stiff upper lip. Despite his strange attire he was a very nice young man and was very grateful that I had gone up to see him especially when it proved that his problem was easily resolved. It was just that his passport was pretty well worn and the pages very faded – as though it had been in water and had dried out. The plastic covering on the personal details page of his passport was also a little bit loose. The Immigration Officers were suspicious about the passport in case it was a forgery and just wanted confirmation that he was

British. As soon as I confirmed that the passport was genuine they released him and let him continue with his journey. He was going to Penang but declined my offer of a lift in my hire car and insisted on travelling by bus. I wished him a safe journey and off he went to the bus station. I also suggested before he left that he might like to call into the High Commission when he arrived in KL to get himself a new passport before he continued his travels to other countries – to save himself having similar problems when he crossed other countries borders. He never arrived – maybe one of my colleagues at the British High Commission in Singapore had to go to his assistance when he arrived there.

Chapter 5

I just hoped that he would not have the same problem as another of my Consular cases who had been half way through his round the world trip using local transport in each country when he caught a bus in Thailand which would bring him down to the Malaysian border where he planned to take other buses down to Singapore. This young man had phoned the High Commission and from the tone of his voice I could tell that he absolutely terrified and scared out of his wits, which was hardly surprising after he had told me his story.

It seemed that he had been travelling on a bus in Thailand heading for the Malaysian border when two middle aged respectable looking ladies got on and sat in the two seats in front of him. After a while one of the ladies turned around and started talking to him, asking him where he was from, what he had been doing, where he had been and where he was going – the usual polite sort of conversation. He told me that they seemed very nice ladies and very interested in his travels. Shortly before they reached the stop where they were due to get off the bus – still some miles away from the Malaysian border – they asked him if he would like to break his journey for a few hours and go to their house for tea. They explained that the buses were quite frequent and that he could easily catch the next bus which was due in a couple of hours time. He thought this would be a good idea – and as he had no definite plans he decided that the opportunity to see a proper Thai house and how ordinary people lived was too good to miss – so he agreed.

They got off the bus together and walked a short distance to this lady's house where he sat down with them drinking tea and chatting. Shortly afterwards a man arrived – who was a friend of the two ladies. Apparently he seemed a very pleasant, agreeable sort of chap and was asking the young man where he had been and where he was going next. During their conversation the man told him that he was working locally in some office or other and had quite a responsible job. A little while later he made a phone call to a friend and asked him to come around to meet the young man as well. It was not long after the new friend arrived before the first man suggested that they have a few hands of poker. He explained that he and his friend had devised a system which they were going to use when they went to the casino in the hopes that they would make a big killing and win millions of baht. He hoped that the young man, by joining them in a game, could help them to perfect their system. The young man told me that he tried to refuse by saying that he did not play cards very well or very often, but they assured him that it was just for fun and would a great help to them to see how their system would work with an additional unknown player. The young man, not wanting to be a spoil sport, especially as he was a guest in the house, finally agreed.

A card table was quickly erected and a new deck of cards produced as if by magic. Large wads of money were placed on the table and divided equally amongst the players. He was assured that the game was not for real but that they needed to have money rather than buttons or matchsticks to make it seem real. Well initially the young man was nervous but when he started winning he started to relax a little bit. It wasn't long though before his winning streak ended, and he started to lose, finally ending up losing all the money he had been given. He said that he tried to pull out of the game at that stage but was told not to worry – he was helping them perfect their system and they gave him some more money to use for his bets.

After a couple of hours playing the game was finally declared over – and then came the crunch - they told him that he owed them the equivalent of GBP2,000. He was absolutely flabbergasted, and reminded them that it was supposed to be a fun game to help them to perfect their system for beating the casino. They were having none of it and told him in no uncertain terms that they would kill him if he did not pay his debt. He was terrified and in fear for his life, so he allowed himself to be escorted to a local bank and withdrew as much money from the ATM as his credit card would allow. Once he had handed over the equivalent of about GBP500 he was then taken to a travel agency where he was forced to purchase two tickets to the Philippines which he duly did. After he had done this he was told that they were going to let him go but had better not tell anyone about it, especially the police, or else they would find him and kill him.

He caught the next bus to the border and crossed over into Malaysia. Even then he did not feel safe and decided that he had to tell someone about it – just in case they were following him to demand more money or airplane tickets from him – or even worse - carry out their threat to kill him – so he telephoned the High Commission. I tried to put his mind at rest by saying that they would not do this and suggested that he come down to Kuala Lumpur to the High Commission as quickly as possible. He said that he was coming to KL but was heading straight to the airport to catch a flight back to the UK – he had had enough of travelling. This experience had totally destroyed all of his confidence and he was abandoning his plans to journey around the rest of the world. I asked him to give me a call once he arrived and was in the airport – which he did and told me he had a seat on a BA flight that evening. I presume he arrived back in the UK safe and sound because I never heard from him again. I would imagine it will be a long time before he resumes his travels overseas especially after such a harrowing experience. It just goes to show – when you are travelling alone – be careful who you befriend or who you allow to befriend you. Watch out for what appears to be respectable middle aged ladies on buses – especially in Thailand.

Chapter 6

Another prison visit I used to make on a regular basis during my first year in Malaysia was to a Chinese/Malay lady in Kajang prison in Selangor some distance outside of Kuala Lumpur – famous for its Kajang Satays. She was a British Passport holder having previously been married to a British National and had lived in the UK for a number of years before returning to Malaysia after her husband died. She was a con artist. Apparently, after she had returned, she had been conning local people by telling them that she was a Bomoh (a sort of Malaysian witchdoctor come psychic healer who helps people by bringing benefits to all who came into contact with them). She was claiming to have special magical powers and could turn stones into gold nuggets. Some of the locals believed her and started bringing her lumps of stone and paying her a hefty fee so that she could – over a period of time – turn the stone into gold. Needless to say – given her present situation – it did not take long, when the gold nuggets did not materialise, before someone reported her to the police. She was subsequently tried, found guilty and sentenced to a few years in prison.

The prison was quite a way out of town – about a 45 minute drive. When I arrived I was directed to the female section of the prison and after showing some identification was allowed to go in. I was not going to be allowed to meet her privately in a separate room but had to go into a long communal visiting hall where there were lots of little windows – rather like the windows in a bank or post office – prisoners were at one side of the glass and visitors on the other side. A telephone was provided at each window so that the prisoners and their visitors could talk to each other. She was a cheerful soul who I could tell was well liked by her fellow inmates and staff alike – everyone seemed to know her. When she came into the interview area she always put her hand up on her side of the glass and I did the same at my side – the only handshake we were allowed to make. She had actually completed her sentence a year or more before I started visiting her but because she was going to be deported she had to provide the prison authorities with some address of where she would go. She had been refusing to do this for a long time and seemed very happy to remain in prison. She was being fed and watered and seemed to have a pretty free hand of where she went in the prison and what she did – I suppose that came as a result of her having already completed her sentence. My boss John had been trying to convince her for months before I arrived that she ought to give the address of the house she owned in the UK to the prison authorities but she had refused to do so. I tried to convince her of the benefits of such a move on my first visit but she steadfastly refused. I was not sure what scam she had going in prison – maybe she was up to her old Bomoh tricks again, but whatever it was she was doing it must have been worth her while staying in there.

The upshot was – after almost a year of me visiting her every month - that one day, out of the blue, she told me when I arrived for one of my visits, that she had decided that she wanted to return to the UK. I was delighted. It was a long time in coming but finally she had seen the light. It was with a mixture of happiness and sadness that we said farewell to each other – we had become quite friendly throughout the time I visited her. But at least she was leaving the prison under her own steam.

Unlike the prisoner my counterpart from the Australian Embassy had been visiting during the first couple of years he was in Kuala Lumpur. It was a case which had been widely reported by the world's press about how an Australian national had been caught with drugs in his possession entering Malaysia. Malaysia has the mandatory death penalty for such offences. He had been tried and sentenced to death. All the appeals over several years had failed and so it was just a matter of time when the execution was to take place. My colleague had been visiting him every month for about 2 years and they had become very friendly with each other. Finally the day came around when the prisoner was to be executed. The Australian Vice Consul was obliged to attend as a witness which must have been an awful experience for him – he had still not got over it when he told me about it – and I suppose he never will.

Chapter 7

In August 1991, not too long after I had arrived in Malaysia, I read in the newspaper one morning that a British National, James Barclay, who was a writer, had been deported from East Malaysia and designated as a 'prohibited visitor' for allegedly filming a group indigenous locals (Penans) who were protesting about the government logging activities in East Malaysia. We were not even aware that he had been detained. By the time I read about it in the newspaper he had already left the country so there was not much I could do about it.

A few months later however, in February 1992, I read in the newspaper that he had once again be detained after entering the country under a different name using a different passport. The Malaysian authorities were not very happy about this and thought that the British government was somehow involved – especially considering he had a brand new passport under a different name. I explained that in UK it is possible for a person to change their name by deed poll or even by placing an advertisement in the newspaper stating that with effect from a certain date they would be known under a new name. The Malaysian authorities seemed a bit doubtful about this and I suspect secretly harboured a suspicion that it was not true.

James Wilson, as he was calling himself then, was in prison just outside Miri so I packed a bag and flew over to see him. Contrary to what appeared in the UK press after he arrived back in the UK, that he had been tortured and deprived of food, he told me that he had been well treated but had been questioned about how he obtained a new name and a new passport. Whether he was saying that he was being well treated to me – just because he was still in prison and did not want incur the wrath of the prison guards – it is hard to say. The officer in charge of the prison however, gave me a different story of what James had been doing in East Malaysia on this visit. He told me that James had been seducing young ladies in the longhouses around that area and this was one of the reasons why they had detained him. <u>Whether this was true or not,</u> I had no way of knowing. The main problem, as far as the Malaysian authorities were concerned, was that he had entered the country again under a different name after being designated a prohibited visitor. When he was deported in the middle of March it was alleged that some young lady from one of the longhouses, came to see him off carrying a baby claiming that it was his.

Some years later, after reading James' book – 'A Stroll through Borneo' and 'Stranger in the Forest; On Foot Across Borneo' by Eric Hansen, I was inspired to take the boat trip from Sibu to Kapit and then from Kapit to Balaga and from there to try and get deeper in the Jungle to visit some remote long houses if possible. It was a spectacular trip up the fast flowing Rajang River, which at 563 km is the longest river in Malaysia, but I was a little bit disappointed by my mode of transport. I had expected to be on a long open boat with outboard motors at the back but this boat was a jet boat – which strongly resembled the fuselage of an aircraft. It was very fast and had air-conditioning inside and a large television screen which showed Chinese style Kung Fu movies throughout the whole 2 hour journey up to Kapit – much enjoyed by all my fellow passengers who probably did not have television in their homes. Kapit is a small town on the south side of the river which was founded in 1880 by Rajah Charles Brooke as a garrison town primarily to prevent the Iban from migrating up-river to attack Orang Ulu settlements. I stayed there overnight so that I could have a look around before catching the boat to Balaga next morning. The hotel in Kapit was pretty dismal really more like a doss house than a hotel. My room was up some filthy stairs and the bed looked as though the sheets hadn't been changed in weeks, but at least I had somewhere to rest my head.

The following morning I took another jet boat up to Balaga which had to negotiate the treacherous Pelagus rapids which are about 6 kilometres long. Rather than be cooped up inside the boat for 3 or 4 hours with the air-conditioning and the Kung Fu movies I decided I would sit on the top of the boat and get some sun. It was fantastic – watching the boat manoeuvring up the rapids and also the activity of other small boats along the river as they went about their daily tasks – some fishing and some just zipping about the water. We even stopped at a remote little kampong (village) – one of many dotted alongside the river – to deliver some letters.

What really amazed me though about the trip up the Rajang river, was the amount of logs which were being transported by boat or piled high on the banks of the river waiting to be transported. It looked as though half of the rain forest must have been chopped down. I began to understand then why some people are concerned about the deforestation of East Malaysia.

Balaga was an even smaller town than Kapit but I was given a guided tour of the town by a very kind young man who took me all over on the back of his motor bike. I stayed overnight and took him out for dinner that evening in one of the little cafe/ restaurants. I had been hoping to go even further up river and deeper into the interior to visit the long houses of the Orang Ulu tribes but I could not get a permit from the local police station so sadly I had to turn back. It was a shame because the open boats used for this final leg of my journey were long narrow boats, the kind of boats I had been expecting to travel in from Sibu. Feeling a little bit disappointed I made my way back to Sibu again. I was pleased with what I had seen – it was just that I wanted to see more.

Chapter 8

Immigration interviews can be quite rewarding at times – not in the financial sense I must add – just in case any reader may get the wrong impression and think I was taking bribes. I remember one Chinese Malaysian girl who came in to apply for her student visa so that she could go to the UK to study for her ACCA (Accounts qualifications). She already had ACCA 1 and 2 but wanted to study for ACCA level 3. When I looked at her documents it became apparent that she did not meet the criteria for a student visa because the course she had enrolled on was not for at least 15 hours of study per week – so she did not qualify. Well when I told her the bad news that I was going to have to refuse her visa application she burst into tears and started sobbing her little heart out. I apologised once again and after handing her the notice of refusal asked her to leave the interview room, which she seemed reluctant to do. I therefore decided that if I left the interview room and she was on her own for a little while she could compose herself before going back out into the general waiting area. Well 20 minutes went by and when I looked back into the interview room through the little glass window on the door, she was still in there crying her eyes out. I gave it another 10 minutes and then went back in and asked her what the problem was. She replied that I didn't understand how important this course was to her career. I asked her if she would like to tell me about it in more comfortable surrounding – not through the glass which separated us in the interview room. She agreed so I invited her to join me in the Consular interview room next door which was quiet and had a couple of easy chairs in it. As soon as she had settled down she started telling me all about her problems. It seems that she was working for a very well known International Bank, instructing new members of staff on banking procedures and had been doing this for a number of years. The reason why she wanted the ACCA level 3 qualification was because all of the people she had trained over the years, who were mainly Bumiputras (true Malay – sons of the soil) were, in a matter of months of receiving their training, being promoted to more senior positions than what she held herself. She had asked her boss how she could get promotion and he had explained, because she was not a Bumiputra, she had to have much higher qualifications than the rest. I felt very sorry for this young lady and explained how she could get around her visa problem. A couple of weeks later she came back to the High Commission to apply again for her student visa – armed with a new offer letter which complied with the Immigration Rules requirements for students. I authorised her visa and said to her "don't let me down now – work hard and get your ACCA level 3'. She assured me that she would.

It was 6 months later when she came back to the High Commission with her ACCA level 3 certificate, plus an article from the Times newspaper which listed her name as having passed the course – and last but not least - a large cake for me to say 'thank you'. The last I heard from her was a couple of weeks later when she telephoned to say that she had just been promoted and was being transferred to their branch in Penang. I was delighted for her. It was, and still is, a pleasure and a very satisfying feeling to be able to help someone to improve their life's chances.

On the subject of telephone calls, we received quite an amusing telephone call one day from a Yorkshire girl with a very strong Yorkshire accent, which has much flatter almost guttural vowels. It seems that she was on holiday in Malaysia and had been visiting various cities seeing the sights. Whilst she was in Kuala Lumpur she had gone into a large church to have a look around – and I suspect cool down a bit from the heat and humidity. Well whilst she was in there a young, handsome looking priest came up to her and offered to show her around – which she gladly accepted. During the tour of the church it seems that the priest took her to some dark corner in the cloisters and started to kiss her. She said, in her very strong Yorkshire accent which I can't replicate on paper "he started to kiss me and then he put his tongue into my mouth – it's not right for a man of the cloth to do something like that". I asked what she did next and she said that she left the church and went outside – but then she told me that she decided that she would go back in again. When she got back inside she went up to the priest, supposedly to remonstrate with him, he kissed her again and again put his tongue in her mouth. When I asked her why she went back in she said "well he was very handsome and I liked it". I invited her to come to the High Commission if she wanted to make a formal complaint but she said she was in another city and the incident had happened a few days earlier. I was not really sure why she had taken the time to telephone to report the incident maybe there is some truth in that old Yorkshire saying "There's nowt so queer as folk".

Chapter 9

Another morning of checking the newspapers revealed that a group of about 8 foreign nationals had been arrested in Miri after chaining themselves to various pieces of machinery in the jungle in protest at what they considered to be excessive logging activities in East Malaysia. A couple of them were British and were due to appear in court with the rest of the group the following day. I quickly packed a bag and booked a flight to Miri for that afternoon. After my previous experience of staying at the Park Hotel – I was going to avoid it like the plague. I checked the list of other hotels which were available in Miri and made a reservation for a room in the Gloria Hotel which proved to be a much nicer hotel. It was also conveniently situated in the centre of town closer to the restaurants and bars and the court house.

Upon arrival in Miri I checked into the hotel and was surprised to see Axel, the Swedish Vice Consul who by coincidence, was also staying at the same hotel. It seems that some members of the protest group were Swedish so he had also dashed over to Miri to be present at the court hearing the following morning.

We decided, because it was still quite early that we ought to wander down to the beach area and have a few drinks. Well the few drinks turned into many and by about 9pm, Axel was feeling a little bit worse for wear and decided, after being violently sick on the pavement, that he would return to the hotel to have a rest and be ready for the court session the following morning. I wasn't feeling too bad and decided to have a nightcap in a bar quite close to the hotel. As I was walking back to the hotel I was approached by 2 beautiful looking girls – who asked me what I was doing and would I like them to accompany me to my hotel room. Well it sounded like it might be an interesting experience and my imagination was running wild, until just before we got to the hotel they informed me that they were not girls at all but men. I could hardly believe it – they looked so beautiful - anyway I bade them farewell and wished them luck in finding someone who might be interested in whatever it was they were offering.

The following morning Axel and I were at the court house bright and early ready for the hearing before the judge. The courthouse was a rather old fashioned colonial looking single storey white wooden building which looked as though it may have been built during the time of Charles Brooke, the white rajah of Sarawak. We stood around waiting for a while before the prisoners arrived in a police van, just moments before the hearing was due to start. Once they got out we had the chance to talk to them briefly to ask how they were being treated before they were led into the court house. Axel and I along, with a few journalists, trooped into the court behind them and sat down listening to the charges, waiting to hear what the verdict was going to be.

During the course of the hearing my eyes were drawn to one of the court officials standing close by the female protesters. She was extremely beautiful even in her court robes, honey coloured skin, and beautiful almond shaped eyes with long eyelashes, sensual lips and jet black hair in a page boy hair style, not to mention her fantastic figure. It was love at first sight. My eyes seemed to take on a life of their own and kept returning to look at her throughout the whole of the hearing. Sadly once the hearing was over she disappeared to the back of the court and I didn't think I would ever see her again. The hearing was adjourned within about an hour until the following week so that the protestors could instruct lawyers to act on their behalf.

About a week later, Axel and I flew back over to Miri again to attend the court hearing with the lawyers who had been engaged by the protesters. The lawyers were looking very splendid in their grey suits, white shirts, ties and black gowns – especially considering the heat and humidity. The judge for this hearing was a lot older than the previous one and didn't seem to have much time for one of the young Chinese lawyers and kept reminding him that he did not have to keep proving how learned he was each time he spoke by referring to similar cases from law books and articles which he had read. The case went on for a couple of days and eventually the protestors were sentenced to a few more days in prison before being deported. I had been hoping that I would see the beautiful court official again during the second hearing but much to my disappointment she was not present in court this time.

Chapter 10

Not long after the court case, my boss informed me that it was time for me to make another Consular trip to East Malaysia. This time the trip was to include Kuching, Miri, Kota Kinabalu, Sandakan and Tawau. It was to be about a 7 day trip altogether. The trip to Sandakan was to inspect a couple of Hong Kong fishing boats which had been detained in Sandakan for over 12 months for illegally fishing in Malaysian waters. Hong Kong was still a British colony at that time, until 1997, so we had Consular responsibilities for Hong Kong nationals. Lots of letters had been exchanged between the High Commission and the local Port authorities in Sandakan but the boats were still being detained. I was to go along to see what was happening and also have a look at the boats to see if they were still in good order. I was also to visit Tawau on the south eastern tip of Sabah to inspect the war memorial in honour of the British servicemen who had died there during the second world war fighting the Japanese and hold a Consular clinic.

The visit to Kuching was short and sweet – only one day and I collected quite a few student visa and visit visa applications. Next stop Miri where once again I met Bill Fowler out at the Petronas complex. After I had finished my consular clinic he invited me back to his house so that he could get changed before we went out for a drink and some dinner. As we arrived at his house, Pauline, his wife, had just arrived in her car and was pulling into their driveway. To my amazement who should get out of the passengers side of her car but the beautiful court official I had seen in the court some weeks earlier. I could not believe my luck. She was even more stunning out of her court robes and in her ordinary clothes. I was completely swept off my feet and couldn't take my eyes off her and I got the feeling that she felt the same way about me. I tried to suggest that we all go out for dinner together but she (Jane) said she was married and had to go home to see her children and husband. Bill told me later that both his wife and Jane were from the Bidayuh tribe (formally a tribe of headhunters), which was a little bit worrying – I knew I was head over heels in love with her but I did not really want to lose my head. I tried to get her phone number but she was not very receptive to that request but cupid's arrow was firmly imbedded in my heart – I would just have to see her again somehow – I was well and truly smitten. Early next morning I flew up to Kota Kinabalu.

Eventually after my day's consular clinic in Kota Kinabalu and another enjoyable evening with our warden at the Yacht Club, I arrived in Sandakan to inspect the two fishing boats. After checking in to the hotel I found out where they were berthed and headed off down to the harbour. I had expected to see just small fishing boats but these were enormous ocean going trawlers (almost as big as HMS Plover) and they had some amazing equipment on the bridge which must have cost a small fortune including a Satellite navigation system and special sonar equipment to help them find the fish. The Captain told me that the fish they caught were worth an awful lot of money in the Hong Kong fish market. After having a good look around both boats to check that they were still seaworthy, I bade farewell to the Captain and said that I would be writing another letter to the port authorities when I returned to KL to ask when they were going to be released. It took a few more letters but eventually they were allowed to return to Hong Kong a couple of months later.

My next port of call was at the office of the local lawyer who had been assisting us with the case. He was a very charming young Chinese man who explained the latest position and what action we needed to take next before suggesting that we have lunch with his wife followed by a visit the Orang Utan rehabilitation centre which was just outside of town.

As planned he and his wife came to collect me at my hotel and after a delicious lunch in the restaurant of a beautiful hotel on the hillside they drove me to the Orang Utan rehabilitation centre at Sepilok. The centre is a short drive out of town and it is here that young orang utans who have either been abandoned by their mother at an early age or rescued by the staff from the centre after being held in cages in remote villages by villagers who sometimes capture them and keep them as pets are rehabilitated. Once they are able to fend for themselves they are released back into the rain forest again. Some of them I was told arrive at the centre in a very sorry state, especially those who have been kept as pets in a cage. It was wonderful to see them coming to the feeding stations both on foot and swinging through the trees and to see the wardens feeding them bananas and even coconuts which the older orang utans were bashing against the tree trunks to crack open so that they could drink the milk inside.

There were 2 feeding stations in the Sepilok reserve. We watched the feeding taking place at one station and then decided to walk down to the other feeding station to see what was going on there. As I was walking down the narrow footpath, just ahead of the Chinese lawyer and his wife, towards the next feeding station there was a young orang utan (who I later found out was called Bobby) walking towards me. He was looking at me and I was looking at him. Just as we were passing each other he suddenly jumped up into my arms and threw one arm over my shoulder and rested his head on my shoulder. I was very surprised and not sure what I should do so I started bouncing him in my arms like a baby. Lots of other tourists thought it was part of the show and started taking photographs. I was happy to be holding him and he also seemed to be enjoying himself but then he got hold of my left hand and put my little finger, which has a signet ring on it, into his mouth. It was then that I started to get a little bit worried just incase he bit it off and my little finger and ring disappeared into his stomach. I wasn't sure that my insurance company would believe my claim that an orang utan had eaten my finger and ring so I decided to let go of him. He dropped to the ground quite easily and scampered off to the feeding station we had just left. He left his calling card – a large dirty handprint on the back of my clean white T shirt.

That evening I was in the hotel having a drink in the bar when I met a Scotsman (Jim) who had lived in Sandakan for years. Although he seemed to be a bit of a lounge lizard we spent a couple of hours chatting together. He was telling me that he had been in Sandakan for a long, long time and was married to a local lady. He said that he had his own little timber company - not a very large company – more of a one man band really. It seems that he used to go into the rain forest every once in a while and saw down a tree and then sell the timber. The money he got from selling the timber would probably last him for between 6 months and a year.

His existence did not sound all that good really. He told me that he owned a house, which his wife and her brother lived in, but he was not allowed into the house, but lived and slept in a shed in the garden – strange arrangement. During the course of our conversation he told me about the island of Sipadan which he said is a diver's paradise not too far away from the coast line. He suggested that I might like to go there the next day if I had time. Well the thought of a trip on the ocean to visit a beautiful island which is shaped like a mushroom was too good to resist.

Early next morning we drove to Semporna, a town a little bit further south, where we were met by a Chinese guy who owned a small wooden narrow boat which had an outboard motor on the back. We piled into the boat, which had no seats, and crouched on the bottom of the boat, which was so narrow that my backside was touching the sides. It was fine whilst we were in the harbour but once we got into the open sea – the boat started to leak and water was coming over the bow. Was this such a good idea after all I was asking myself – we started to bail in earnest with little plastic cups. As if this was not bad enough – after about an hour in the boat – without any life jackets or anything like that and no land in sight anywhere – the driver of the boat suddenly informed us that these waters were notorious for pirates. Just what I wanted to hear - I really did begin to wonder then whether this trip had been such a good idea after all.

Sipadan Island is quite a small island which rises 600 metres from the seabed and is located in the Celebes Sea, east of Tawau. It was formed over thousands of years by living coral growing on the top of an extinct volcano cone. The beach all around the island is about 5 metres or so wide and once you go any further than that it is a straight drop of 600 metres to the bottom of the ocean. Truly a diver's paradise – which explains the existence of the Borneo Divers camp at one end of the island.

We stayed on the island overnight, had a drink and some dinner in the diver's camp and slept in a small fisherman's hut on stilts along the beach some distance from the diver's camp. The hut was about the size of a small beach chalet at a seaside resort in UK. I was on the veranda and my Scottish companion and boat driver inside the hut. Just as we were turning in for the night the driver of the boat said that he had seen a female turtle coming ashore to lay her eggs in the sand. He suggested that we walk along the beach to watch. We took a couple of flash lights with us and watched in amazement as she finished digging the hole and then proceeded to lay what seemed like hundreds of soft table tennis ball sized eggs. Once she had finished she carefully covered the eggs with sand and headed back to the sea again. The driver of the boat marked the spot where she had laid her eggs and said that he would be back next day to collect some of them.

Next morning he did just that and dug up the sand where the turtle had laid the eggs and filled a couple of buckets with eggs before covering the remaining eggs with sand again so that they could hatch. When I asked him if it was allowed to remove the eggs, he told me that he had been given permission to collect turtle eggs from the island and that he sold them in town for a very good price. I was not entirely convinced but because we were relying upon him to take us back – I decided it was best not to say anything.

The journey back was exactly the same as the trip out – we were bailing for most of the two and a half hours it took us to get back to the harbour. In some ways I wished we had taken the speed boat which went roaring by us as it was ferrying the Borneo Divers clients to and from Sipadan in about 30 minutes. But on reflection I decided – once we were safely back on terra firma again - that the uncertainty of the journey in the narrow boat was much more exciting.

Chapter 11

Once we arrived back in Sandakan I caught a flight to Tawau which is another small town, quite close to the Indonesian border on the South Eastern tip of Sabah. The purpose of the visit was to go and have a look at the War Memorial to British Servicemen who had served and died in that area during the war and also to hold a Consular clinic. The war memorial when I saw it was not in a very good state of repair and the ground around it was quite untidy. I took a couple of photographs and headed back to my hotel.

As soon as I got back to my room I telephoned our contact in Tawau who turned out to be the Commodore of the Tawau Yacht Club. He duly invited me to join him in the club that evening to have dinner and a few drinks. The Club, when I got there, was a very splendid, old fashioned club where nearly all the members seemed to have bottles of spirits behind the bar with their names on. As the Commodore told me – the only problem with this system is that you realise how much you are drinking when you get your bill at the end of the month listing how many bottles you have consumed that month.

During the evening's conversation I mentioned that I had met the Scottish guy in Sandakan – and everyone seemed to know Jim or at least heard of him. The commodore told me that a few years earlier a Scottish lady who said that she was Jim's sister had arrived in Kota Kinabalu making enquiries about her brother – trying to find out where he was. Apparently Jim got wind on the grapevine of the fact that this lady might be heading to Sandakan to find this long lost brother and quickly vanished into the rain forest for a couple months until he heard that she had left and it was safe to come out. He was adamant that this lady was not related to him – but nevertheless he did a vanishing act for a while – so everyone suspected that she must be some sort of relation - maybe even his British wife....

Anyway it was a very enjoyable evening in the yacht club and the company was excellent. Feeling in good spirits and full of the joys of spring I decided to walk the 2 miles or so back to the hotel but little did I know that I would be walking through a pretty dodgy area of town – no one in the yacht club told me about it until the next day – which was too late.

The dodgy area was badly lit and a little bit rundown but full of little restaurants and bars. It was also not too far from the hotel – probably about half a mile. By the time I reached there I had worked up quite a thirst and decided to stop off for a nightcap – because the bar in the hotel would be closed at that time of night. I found a little bar which seemed very quiet and went in. It was empty apart from a couple of girls behind the bar. Within a few minutes of me sitting down – one of the girls - a very pretty girl - came and sat next to me and we started chatting. A little bit later a group of 5 or 6 young men came in and it became pretty obvious they were watching me talking to this girl. Well just as I was leaving – the group of young men, who must have decided that I had been talking to one of their girlfriends for far too long, followed me outside, and formed a semi circle around me. I tried to tell them that I was harmless and was just going back to my hotel when they decided that I needed to be taught a lesson. One of them had what looked like a miniature railway sleeper in his hand and a couple of others had handfuls of what looked like half-bricks. I could see what was going to happen so I took my glasses off and put them on the window ledge of the building which was behind me. The guy with the railway sleeper came at me first and tried to whack me at the side of my chest. Luckily I managed to bring my arm down as he did so and was able to wrench the railway sleeper from his grasp. Now I had the railway sleeper – things looked a bit better, as far as I was concerned. The youths with the bricks started to throw them at me and I ended up using the railway sleeper as a cricket bat and was batting the bricks back at them whilst at the same time keeping on the move. My days of playing cricket at Bingley Grammar School hadn't been wasted. Within a few minutes all of them except the guy who had been using the railway sleeper decided enough was enough and they vanished. As soon as he realised that he was on his own and that I was walking towards him looking very menacing, with the railway sleeper in my hands, he also decided that enough was enough and ran off as well. I was very lucky and thanked my lucky stars that I only had a graze on the side of my forehead where one of the bricks had caught me – I obviously needed to practice my cricket hook shots. My glasses somehow got broken and I had to phone the High Commission in KL to send my spare pair over as quickly as possible. When I mentioned this to the Commodore when he came to see me the next day at the Consular Clinic he said "we should have told you to get a taxi and not to walk through that area – it can be quite dangerous". I just wished he had. When I got back to KL I had to write a report on what had happened and we also amended our travel advice for British tourists visiting Tawau.

Chapter 12

Life in KL was anything but dull – there always seemed to be something happening. Besides being busy in the office I was still playing lots of tennis and jogging on a regular basis. One day a British girl came in to see me to complain that her Malaysian husband was always beating her and would not allow her to go out of the house on her own and had even confiscated her passport to prevent her from leaving him and returning to the UK. She convinced me that she was in serious danger if she continued living with her husband and asked if we could assist her to get back to the UK. I asked her to try to come back the following day and bring some passport sized photographs so that we could issue her with another passport. Her previous passport had been issued in KL so there was no problem about us checking her nationality. We arranged a flight and because she had no money we lent her some money to pay for her new passport and her air ticket - after she had signed an undertaking to repay the amount in full once she was back in the UK.

A couple of days later everything was arranged, the flight and the passport. We gave her strict instructions to go to the airport and not tell anyone what she was doing – just incase they told her husband. We also advised her to check in as soon as she arrived at the airport so that she could get airside where she would be safer – rather than be on the landside of the airport where she may be seen by someone. It just so happened that I was also at the airport that evening – meeting someone who had just arrived. I was shocked to see the girl sauntering around the airport because she seemed to be in no hurry whatsoever to check in as we had advised her to do. When she saw me she came running over and wanted to chat but I quickly ushered her towards the check in desk and finally got her airside where she would be safer.

Well we thought that was the last we would see of her, but lo and behold, about 6 weeks later she came back to the High Commission again seeking our assistance to return to the UK. It seems that when she got back to the UK she decided that she was missing her husband and thought she should come back to Kuala Lumpur to be with him because she felt sure that he would be behave differently towards her this time. It wasn't long though, before the beatings and the imprisonment in the house started again. She said that she had sneaked out of the house this time through a window so that she could come to the High Commission to request our assistance again to go back to the UK. As cruel as it may seem, I'm afraid we had to disappoint her. She had not re-paid the first loan so we had to tell her that she would have to do that first before we could give her any more money, alternatively she should approach her family or friends for funds to pay for her ticket this time. I think she abandoned the idea of returning to the UK and is probably still in Kuala Lumpur – although I hope she is not still being beaten and imprisoned.

Chapter 13

Not long after this, another case of a distressed girl, this time a Malaysian girl, came to my attention when she and her British husband came to the High Commission, to apply for her settlement visa so that she could travel with him to the UK and settle there. They both came in to the interview room together initially and the British guy told me that they had recently got married and that they would like to return to UK to live there. He explained that he was a retired senior British army officer and that he had his own house in the UK. He was financially sound because he had his army pension and a part time job as well, so he could easily afford to take care of his new wife when she arrived in the UK.

I thanked him for his introduction and asked him if he would leave the room so that I could interview his wife in private.

As soon as he had left the room and before I really got started with his wife's interview she started telling me how they met and what had happened to her since. My antennas were raised immediately because it did not seem as straight forward as her husband had explained to me.

She said that her husband had placed an advertisement in a local newspaper in East Malaysia (The Borneo Post) saying that he was an ex-British Army officer looking for a wife and that he would be able to take care of them in his house in the UK. It seems he got quite a number of responses to his advert and after a selection period he chose the lady who was sat in front of me and they married a couple of weeks after they first met. She told me that before they were married he had been the perfect English gentleman and that they had stayed in a nice hotel. He was very kind to her and was buying gifts for her and her parents and taking her out for dinners – he seemed like an ideal future husband – her Prince Charming.

As soon as they were married however, things changed drastically. He started beating her and torturing her by putting lighted cigarettes on her breasts – unbelievable. She said this had been going on for a week or more before they came to KL for the interview and that she did not want to go with him to the UK. She begged me not to issue her with a visa – needless to say I was happy to oblige.

When I called the husband in and informed him that I was refusing his wife's settlement visa and told him that his wife did not support the entry clearance application, his face dropped and he looked extremely embarrassed. I did not tell him why, just in case he took it out on his wife after they left the visa section – but I am sure he knew. I did however show him the section in the Immigration Rules which said that reluctant spouses should not be issued with a settlement visa.

I hope he did not inflict any more brutality on his wife after they left the visa section and that he never did find a lady from any country to torture as he had done with this lady.

Chapter 14

Some weeks later I received a letter which was written in pencil on a dirty piece of paper and the writing was hardly legible. The letter, which was printed in capital letters, said that the writer was British and was in prison in Johor Baru in the south of Malaysia, just across the water from Singapore. He said he was worried that he would never get out because no one knew he was there. He had written his name at the bottom of the note but no address of the prison was given. I was not sure whether it was a hoax or not but I telephoned the police in Johor Baru, just in case, to ask them if they knew anything about this man. I struck lucky with my first phone call – the police officer I spoke to remembered this man and told me that he was not in prison but was in a hospital on the outskirts of JB. I made arrangements to fly down the following day.

Once I arrived at the Police Station I was then taken by police car and dropped off at the hospital. The lady on reception did not seem to know much about this man or where he was so she called one of the Doctors. When the Doctor arrived, he told me that this young man was one of his patients and that he would take me to see him. I asked him what was wrong with the young man and he just said that he was a little bit disturbed. It was a large modern hospital with lots of grassy areas all around the wards and administration buildings. We walked for quite a long way, leaving all the buildings and wards behind us, before arriving at what can best be described as a sort of stockade. There was a tall white wall with barbed wire and broken glass on the top surrounding a building which I could just see the top of behind the wall. As we approached the metal gates to the stockade I could see that they were as high as the wall and were securely closed – with a hefty looking chain and a large padlock. I said to the Doctor – 'don't tell me – my man is in here isn't he' to which he replied 'yes'.

Almost as soon as we got inside the gates, we became surrounded by patients – all of whom seemed to be drugged up to the eyeballs. The lights were on but nobody was at home. The doctor was wearing his white coat and I was in my suit carrying a brief case and so the patients assumed that I was also a doctor. A group of them gathered around me and were saying 'hello doctor' to me when suddenly I felt someone fondling my backside. I looked at the doctor and he smiled, as if to say 'it wasn't me and it always happens in here' We got inside the building as fast as we could make our way through the patients who milling all around us and I was taken to a grubby little room where I found a British man lying on the floor – also looking heavily sedated. The doctor gently told him I was from the British High Commission and that I had come to help him so that he could return to the UK. He seemed to wake up at hearing this and was able to talk to me. He told me that he knew he had some psychiatric problem but when he was in JB it had become worse and he had been acting very strangely and that is why he had been detained by the police and eventually put in the hospital. He thought he had been there for a couple of months at least. I asked him about his family in the UK and where they lived and he gave me some contact details. I told him that I would have to go back to KL to arrange for someone in the FCO to contact his family to ask them to provide him with an air-ticket so that he could go back to the UK. He seemed a bit worried about this because he was not sure whether his family would be prepared to help him or not. I assured him that we would try our best to get them to agree to pay – if not we would find another way to get him home again. This seemed to cheer him up.

When I returned to KL I sent a telegram to the Consular Department of the FCO giving them the guy's details and asked them to contact his parents to explain the situation their son was in. A couple of days later I received a telegram from Consular Department confirming that they had received the money from his family to pay for their son's flight back to the UK. The only problem was that they were leaving for Australia the following day to visit some other relatives so there would be no one at home when he arrived.

I called the hospital and spoke to the Doctor to inform him that we were going to make plans for his patient to fly back to the UK. It would mean a flight from JB up to KL and then a flight from KL to London. I asked the Doctor whether they would be sending a nurse as escort – just in case the guy had another attack whilst he was on the plane. The doctor said that it would not be necessary – they would give him an injection before he left JB and that would keep him calm for about 8 hours or so. I reminded the Doctor that the flight to London from JB would take a lot longer than that – especially as he would have to change flights in KL and wait for the London flight. The Doctor did not seem particularly concerned about this and said that besides giving him an injection they would give him some pills which he could take if he felt an attack coming on. So that is what happened in the end. I purchased the air ticket and sent it down to the hospital and the patient flew back to the UK. I was a little bit worried about him – and for any passengers who might be sat near him – just in case he had another attack during the flight - but apparently he didn't. I am not sure what happened to him when he got home – especially as his family had already left for Australia. I just hoped that he was alright once he was back in familiar surroundings.

Chapter 15

We had an amusing visitor one day to the Consular Section – at least I thought it was amusing.

A middle aged man called in to ask if he could have the personal details of his passport changed. At that time British passports were the old blue/black hardback book passports – sadly missed by some Brits – before the soft digital readable passports came into being. It would have been easy to have amended it because the personal details were handwritten rather than computer generated but we had to be sure before we made any such amendments.

He wanted his title changing from Mr to 'Lord'. In support of his request he produced a certificate which stated that he was now Lord so and so. I assumed it was some sort of joke because the certificate did not look very official even though it had some fancy blue ribbon attached to it and a red seal – it was more like an upmarket version of the kind of certificate you can buy at a seaside resort or in a gift/joke shop which says 'Greatest Dad or Best Wife'. He was quite insistent and said that he wanted it changing as quickly as possible.

Rather than embarrass the poor guy – I said that I would have to take a copy of the certificate and send the details off to London for confirmation of his title and that it would be a few days before we would be able to change his passport. I asked him to call back the following week. Needless to say he never came back to hear the news that his certificate and title were not recognised as being authentic. I assumed he wanted it so that he could either impress people or even use it to commit some sort criminal activity. Whatever reason he wanted it for – we were unable to oblige.

Chapter 16

Our Consular warden in Johor Baru was a retired British Businessman – about 75 years old. He still did a little bit of work for his ex-company and also acted as our representative looking after British Nationals interests in JB, so whilst I was in town seeing the patient in hospital I called in to see him.

He was an extremely nice old boy who loved the game of Rugby. I had played a decent standard of Rugby myself during my time in the Navy and also whilst I was in Darwin so we had lots to talk about. He liked a drink in the afternoons, and John my boss in KL, had warned me before I went down that I had to be careful when I was with Mr Lee. He said that he had been falling down drunk after an afternoon session with him and had to be helped back to his hotel. He also told me that I would be asked about the MBE (Member of the British Empire) recommendation which had been submitted on Mr Lee's behalf.

Well just as John had predicted – off we went to Mr Lee's club, where the drinks were flowing for the whole afternoon, and talked about what Mr Lee called 'the great game' - Rugby. Also as John had predicted – the MBE question was raised. All I could say was that I would look into it when I arrived back in KL.

It was sheer coincidence that a couple of weeks later we received notification from the Honours Department of the FCO informing us that Mr Lee's MBE had been approved. When I gave him the good news he was absolutely delighted. I asked him whether he would like to travel to London to receive it from Queen Elizabeth at Buckingham Palace or whether he would like to have it presented by the High Commissioner in KL at his residence. He said that as much as he would like to meet the Queen he thought he was too old to travel all that way, so opted for a ceremony at the High Commissioner's residence instead.

The ceremony was arranged to take place a few weeks afterwards and Mr Lee arrived in KL with some of his daughters and friends, so that they could share this special moment with him. The ceremony was very successful with the High Commissioner making a very nice speech about what Mr Lee had done to earn his MBE and how grateful we were for all of his help during the many years he had been our Consular Warden. The High Commissioner had even laid on some drinks and snacks for all the guests. Mr Lee was extremely grateful for all I had done – even though it was very little. He and his family returned to JB the following day but sadly I was not to see him again.

Tragically it was only a matter of weeks after he had received his much coveted MBE that he died. One of his daughters telephoned me to give me the sad news. She said that his funeral and cremation had been arranged and would be taking place in Singapore a few days later. She also said that he had left instructions in his will that GBP200 was to be placed behind the bar at the Singapore Cricket Club (another of his favourite haunts and games) so that all of his friends could give him an appropriate send-off. I went down to the funeral, as the High Commission representative. The church was full of his friends, relatives and ex colleagues. It was a very moving service but the strange thing was that at the end of the ceremony, the priest asked the congregation whether they would like to observe the body being burnt in the crematorium, which was attached to the side of the church. Some people did but I didn't fancy the idea of watching Mr Lee go up in flames.

Once all the proceedings were over, Mr Lee's daughters came up to me and said that he had made another last request in his will which was that his daughters and me should go to his favourite restaurant (which was more like a little pub) and have his favourite food – sausage and mash with onion gravy. It was a nostalgic affair but his daughters were happy that he had had such a good life and we celebrated his life into the early hours of the next morning. I wonder if they are still in Singapore now – I expect they are.

Chapter 17

Late one afternoon some weeks later, I received a very strange telephone call from a Chinese guy who said that he had a British girl and her Japanese boyfriend as guests in his house. He said that the British girl had been acting very strange as she was boarding her flight to the UK and had eventually been removed from the flight. He had been at the airport that morning when this happened and had very kindly offered them a room for the night in his house, which was not too far away from the airport. He said that he was very concerned about the girl because she had suddenly gone very quiet and was not speaking to anyone. He asked if I could go out to his house to speak to her.

Well, I wasn't really sure what was wrong with the young lady so I telephoned the British High Commission Doctor, who was a very nice elderly British man and was the local Doctor used by the High Commission Staff. I explained the situation to him and asked him if he would accompany me to the house where the British girl and her Japanese boyfriend were staying just in case she had some medical problem. He readily agreed.

Off we went in a High Commission car and eventually arrived at the house in Petaling Jaya – some way from the centre of the city. The local Chinese guy and the Japanese boyfriend were waiting outside of the house for us when we pulled up and invited us in. The Japanese guy explained that his girlfriend had been working in Japan and that is where they had met. They had recently got engaged and were on their way back to the UK, after stopping off in KL for a couple of days, where they planned to get married and set up home together. Whilst boarding the aircraft in KL to fly to the UK his girlfriend had become very distressed and was making a scene and refused to board the aircraft. No amount of persuasion would change her mind, so eventually, as the time of departure came and went for the aircraft, their baggage was off-loaded and the flight left without them. He told us that his girlfriend was in the bedroom upstairs in the house but was not speaking to anyone.

I suggested to the Doctor that he should go up speak to her to see if she had some medical problem. After about 15 minutes, he came down and said that she was still not speaking but there did not appear to be anything physically wrong with her. She was just not being very communicative.

I went up and the same process was repeated. I was asking her questions and she was not replying. I suddenly remembered what the Japanese guy told me about them being engaged and going to the UK to get married, so I asked her if this was the problem. She lifted her face and I could tell by her eyes that this was indeed what was worrying her. I told her that there was no need to be worried about a wedding. If she had changed her mind and did not want to marry her Japanese boyfriend – she was not obliged to do so, just because he had a fiancée visa. I went on to explain that if they had not married within 6 months of him arriving in the UK then he would have to leave the country and return to Japan. This seemed to cheer her up no end and she started telling me about her worries about being married to her boyfriend. Shortly afterwards we both went downstairs and she was chatting to everyone – as if nothing had happened.

The Doctor and I left and the girl and her Japanese boyfriend flew to the UK next morning. Whether they ever got married or not – I have no idea, but whatever she decided to do, she was able to make the decision herself without thinking that her boyfriend's visa meant that she had to marry him.

Chapter 18

I had kept in touch with Bill & Pauline in Miri whilst I was in Kuala Lumpur and had always enquired about Jane each time I spoke to them. When my next Consular trip to East Malaysia came around I decided that I would spend just one night in Kuching and fly straight up to Miri at the end of the second day, rather than stay in Kuching for 2 nights. The plan was that I would try and to find some way of seeing Jane whilst I was in Miri overnight.

When I arrived at the airport in Miri, who should be there to meet me, but Pauline and Jane. What a wonderful surprise it was, I couldn't believe my luck. Jane was looking absolutely fantastic even more beautiful than I remembered her – I just wanted to grab hold of her and kiss her. As we were driving back into town Pauline told me that Bill was away for a couple of days on one of the off shore oil drilling platforms but both she and Jane were free for dinner that evening. I felt as though all my birthdays had come at once.

After they had dropped me at the hotel I unpacked and took a shower and changed my clothes and then went down to meet them in the lobby an hour or so later as we had arranged. We had a couple of drinks in the lobby bar and then went into the restaurant to have dinner. After dinner, the three of us went up to my room, where we were chatting for a little while before

Pauline - very diplomatically - announced that she had to go home to make sure her baby was alright and put him to bed. Jane and I were alone at last. Well at first we were both a little bit shy making polite conversation, but before too long we were holding each other and kissing each other – one thing led to another and we were soon lying on the bed – semi clothed. We were like young lovers, hungry for one another, but I think both of us felt that we had come a long way in a very short space of time and did not want to rush things. We did not make love that night but I think we both knew that it would not be long before we did. She stayed with me for quite a while just talking. She told me about her background; that she was from the Bidayuh tribe and had been born in a longhouse in the Padawan district – about 100 kilometres outside of Kuching, quite close to the Indonesian border. She said that she had been hoping to become an air stewardess when she finished her education but that had not worked out and she had joined the Legal services instead. She had married quite young – as I had done – and it seemed that both of us were unhappy with our respective partners. She had three children, a girl and two boys, but her Chinese husband was not very nice to her. I had one wonderful daughter and a wife who was a chain smoking alcoholic. After about an hour she said that she would have to leave – or her husband would begin to wonder where she was and may even phone Pauline's house to see if she was there. As we hugged each other, like there was no tomorrow, we agreed that we must see each other again as soon as I could arrange another trip to Miri. We exchanged telephone numbers on the strict understanding that if I phoned her house and a male voice answered the phone – I should just hang up immediately without saying anything. This was just the beginning. The rest of that particular Consular trip in Kota Kinabalu was conducted in a sort of daze – I don't remember much about what happened after my evening with Jane. All I knew was that I just had to see her again as soon as possible.

Chapter 19

Back in Kuala Lumpur nothing had changed – even though I felt completely different and was phoning Jane on a daily basis – sometimes twice a day. She had given me her home telephone number but she also gave me her office number as well so that I could call her during the day without fear of her husband picking up the phone. I settled in to the Entry Clearance interview routine once again – giving Salina, a British lady who was our locally employed Entry Clearance officer, married to a very nice Malaysian man, some welcome relief. Salina was a very efficient Entry Clearance Officer and I felt sorry in lots of ways leaving her on her own whilst I went on my Consular trips – but she coped very well indeed and had been doing the job for much longer than me.

Soon after I arrived back John, my boss, went up to Penang on a Consular trip for a few days and met up with our Consular Warden up there – John West, who was a retired Senior Partner of a palm oil plantation company but still worked part-time for a few days a week in the company offices. He was the British Consular Warden and also the Swedish Honorary Consul – so he had three jobs altogether, and I must say he did them all very well indeed. We were always allowed to use one of the offices in John's company office for our Consular clinics which were very conveniently located in the centre of town.

Just after John got back to KL, John in Penang telephoned to say that there had been a death of a British national in one of the hotels up there. It seems that a British guy had checked into the hotel and had spent most of his time in his room. Each day the room service were having to completely replenish his Mini Bar because he was emptying it each evening – which was strange because the mini bars in that hotel were particularly well stocked with 3 or 4 miniature bottles each of rum, whisky, brandy, vodka and gin as well as a number of cans of beers and soft drinks. Well on the 4th morning the lady from room service went into his room and found the room empty. She refilled his mini bar as usual and then the house keeping department sent the maid in to clean the room. She was in for the shock of her life.

After she had cleaned the room and the bathroom and made the bed, she went to the wardrobe to get the bedspread to cover the bed and as she opened the door, she found the British guy hanging from the rail with his legs bent at the knee behind him. He had tried to hang himself but had in fact strangled himself with his ties. What a slow and dreadful way to go. The hotel had telephoned John West and told him about what had happened and John arranged for an ambulance to go to the hotel to collect the body. He had also contacted an undertaker to prepare the body for repatriation to the UK once the hospital had carried out an autopsy. He sent a copy of the guy's passport and local death certificate down to us in KL so that we could prepare a British death certificate and report the death to the FCO. The passport was necessary to enable us to find out who his next of kin was and where they lived in the UK so that the Consular Desk officer in the FCO could make arrangements for them to be informed. The Consular Desk Officer in London contacted the local police in that town who sent a policeman around to inform the guy's next of kin of his death and also to enquire if they wanted the body repatriating to the UK or whether they wanted him cremating in Penang. Once all the formalities in the hospital were over and done with – John in Penang arranged for the body to be embalmed and put into a coffin and shipped back to the UK having received approval and payment from the guy's next of kin. We were hardly involved at all.

Another case in Penang where John West once again proved how valuable he was as a Consular Warden was when the body of a British man was found in a quarry at the foot of a very steep, sheer drop. At first it was thought that it was suicide but police investigations proved that there may have been suspicious circumstances surrounding his death. It seems that he had a Chinese girlfriend from Ipoh who had been living with him or at least stayed with him from time to time. When the police went to the man's apartment they found it to be almost completely empty. His joint-bank account was also empty – having had all the funds withdrawn the morning after his death and all of his valuables in his apartment such as his TV, Computer, Hi-fi system and other electrical appliances had been removed. It was suspected that either the girlfriend or some of her male friends from Ipoh had either pushed him or thrown him over the cliff into the quarry. What a tragic way to die. John kept us informed of how the investigations were progressing and also arranged for the body to be returned to his next of kin in the UK – we had a copy of his passport application form in the High Commission so were able to extract these details from there. The body was eventually returned to his family in the UK but the Chinese girl was never found and no one was ever charged with any offence – so we will never know for sure what happened that awful night.

We seemed to have a spate of deaths during that period. One day we received notification of the death of a British man who had been living over in Kuantan on the east coast of the Malaysian peninsula in the state of Pehang. A quick check of the passport application records provided us with the details of his next of kin. His wife in the UK was duly informed about his death and she requested that his body be flown back to the UK for burial, so that she and her children could pay their last respects. Everything seemed to be pretty straightforward until we discovered that he also had a Malaysian wife and children over in Kuantan. His Malaysian wife wanted his body cremating in Malaysia and his ashes to be buried in Kuantan. We had the rather delicate job of telling his British wife that there was another wife and other children in her husband's life which came as a complete shock to her. She said that he had been the most perfect husband, and loving father who had been working in Kuantan for a number of years but made regular trips to their home in the UK every couple of months when his work allowed. The Malaysian wife was also telling us a similar story. He had told her that he had to make business trips to the UK every couple of months but spent most of his time in Kuantan with her and his Malaysian children. It really was a very delicate situation. In the end, the Malaysian wife took the initiative and solved the problem by having his body cremated and ashes buried. Needless to say his wife in the UK was not very happy when she found out but there was nothing we could do about it.

Chapter 20

We had some surprising news one day – we heard that the Queen Elizabeth II – the P & O's flagship cruise liner was going to stop off in Port Kelang – about 60 or so miles away from KL on the West side of the Malaysian Peninsula. It was an unscheduled stop because someone on board had died. They wanted a Consular Officer from the High Commission in Kuala Lumpur to go down to sign the ships log confirming the death. I was happy to go. The last time I had seen the QEII was in the mid 60's when she was being built in John Brown's Shipyard in Clydebank on the River Clyde in Scotland. I had been part of the trials acceptance crew on HMS Intrepid, which was also built by John Brown's Shipyard, whilst she underwent various sea trials in the Clyde and Irish Sea before the Royal Navy accepted her from the ship builders. When I last saw the QEII she only had the hull but no superstructure. It would be interesting to visit her again now she was fully fitted out and operational.

I ordered a High Commission car for that afternoon and the driver drove me down to Port Kelang – about an hour and a half away. When we arrived on the dockside the QEII looked absolutely enormous – much bigger than any Royal Navy ship I had ever been on. I introduced myself to the crew who were manning the gangway and they immediately telephoned the Purser who came to collect me. He was very businesslike and took me straight to his office in the bowels of the ship so that I could sign the ships log. He told me that the man who had died was in his 80's and went on to explain that it was not uncommon for them to have deaths on their cruises and that they always carried a number of coffins to cope with such eventualities. He said that the reason why they had a number of deaths onboard each year was mostly because of passengers overeating. The majority of the passengers he said were older people who could afford such luxuries as a nice cruise on such a beautiful ship. The problem was that most of them, whilst they were onboard, ate a lot more than they normally did. There are 5 meals a day – breakfast, lunch, afternoon tea, Dinner, and a late supper, included in the cost of a cruise and lots of passengers make a point of eating all of them – which is not good for their health. He also said that they have quite a few onboard romances – especially with the older passengers – and that there was one on this particular cruise. The old lady's cabin was absolutely full of red roses – which her admirer was sending to her once and twice per day. How romantic.

After we had finished all the business side of my visit – the Purser kindly showed me all around the ship. She was magnificent, very luxurious with fantastic dining rooms, bars and other entertainment areas. There was even an enormous curved carpeted stairway between two of the decks. It was more like a 5 star hotel than a ship – at least any ship I had been on. What a pleasure it must be to spend a couple of weeks on her cruising around the Indian Ocean – which is generally flat calm, like a mill pond. Maybe one day. I just hope I am not in my 80's by the time that day comes around – or else I might become a Consular case myself and end up in a box after eating too much.

Chapter 21

When I went up to Penang some time later, to be present when one of Her Majesty's warships paid a courtesy visit, I stayed in the centre of town in the Eastern & Oriental Hotel which was and probably still is, a quaint old colonial hotel dating back to when there was a much stronger British presence in Malaysia than there is today. It was a quaint old hotel with old fashioned standards. Most of the staff seemed to be nearly as old as the hotel but the service they offered was very good. The rooms unfortunately not up to today's five star hotel standards but they made up for that in other areas. The food especially was excellent. They served some fabulous breakfasts in the restaurant which included porridge, devil kidneys, kippers, smoked haddock with poached eggs on top and lots of other very British breakfast dishes which are not seen in modern hotels these days.

In the lobby bar that evening there were a couple of old British ladies dressed in 1940's clothes (probably their normal everyday clothes) with old fashioned hair-do's entertaining the guests – one of them played the piano and the other one sang. I suspect that Hinge & Brackett (a two man comedy act in the UK, who dress up as old fashioned ladies, one of whom plays the piano whilst the other one sings) must have stayed there at one time because their comedy act was identical to that of these two old ladies. Neither of them was terribly good, the pianist kept playing wrong notes but it was the singer who was definitely the worst of the two – she had a problem with lots of high notes and was completely out of tune most of the time. It was amusing and pleasant for a little while at least and I had to force myself not to laugh – but after about half an hour my ears could stand it no longer so I decided to go back to my room and read a book and have an early night ready for the cocktail party on Her Majesty's ship the following evening.

As I was walking up the brow (gangplank) of one of Her Majesty's warships behind some other guests, I had just reached the top when I witnessed quite an amusing incident on the crew's brow which was a little bit further forward on the ship than the one which was being used for the cocktail party guests. One of the sailors had come back onboard slightly worse for wear – quite drunk actually - carrying two bottles of whiskey. The officer of the day had been saying to him that bringing spirits onboard one of Her Majesty's warships was not allowed and could get him into trouble. He told the sailor that he was going to turn his back and he wanted to hear two splashes in the water and then nothing more would be said about the incident. Well whilst his back was turned, the sailor quickly removed his shoes and threw them overboard into the water and then started running up the side of the ship in his stocking feet towards a door still clutching his two bottles of whiskey. He was just about to disappear when he was called back and taken away by some other sailors – presumably to be punished the following. Some things never change.

Once I had introduced myself to the officers in the receiving party one of them asked me to follow him to the Captains cabin. I thought this is very impressive - especially as I used to be on the lower deck – being taken to the captain's cabin for a quick drink with him before the party started. I felt very honoured. Well was not to be.

As soon as I entered the Captain's cabin I could tell immediately that something was seriously wrong. The captain and two of his other officers were in there and they all looked shell shocked – and no wonder when they told me what had happened. The captain thanked me for coming and apologised for intercepting me on my way to the cocktail party. He then went on to tell me that one of his officer's wives who had flown out to Penang from the UK with her new baby to spend a couple of days with her husband whilst the ship was in harbour, had thrown herself off the top of the hotel roof. It seemed that she only had arrived that morning from the UK and had been sitting at the side of the pool in the afternoon with her husband and baby. During the course of the afternoon she become increasingly paranoid about mosquitoes biting her baby and was trying to keep it covered up – but was still irritated by them buzzing around. Some time later she said to her husband that she was just going up to their room and would not be long – and that he should take care of the baby and make sure that no mosquitoes got anywhere near it. Well quite a while passed and she had not returned so the husband went to look for her – only to be told that the hotel staff had found her body on the ground at the other side of the hotel. Her body was in an awful mess – the hotel was about 15 stories high. Once her body had been taken to the hospital arrangements were made for the officer and his baby to return to the UK on the same flight as his wife's body. All of the travel plans were arranged by the Royal Navy so we were not really involved. Needless to say I didn't make the cocktail party that night – neither did the captain and the other two officers.

A few weeks later however, we received the lady's wedding ring from the hospital which had been taken off the body during the post mortem examination. It was really knocked out of shape so, we decided, rather than return it to the husband in such a condition we would take it to a local jewellers shop and have it made round again. We hoped by doing this that it would make it easier on the husband to receive it in near perfect condition rather than in the crumpled mess in which it had arrived in our office.

Chapter 22

Shortly after the ship had left Penang I read in the newspaper that a British National (Overseas) – a citizen of Hong Kong - had been detained on the Malaysian border after he had crossed over from Thailand carrying a load of drugs and was currently in prison in Alor Setar awaiting trial. This was very serious indeed – drug trafficking in Malaysia has a mandatory death sentence – with no one spared. I caught a flight up to Alor Setar the following day. The prison looked a lot smaller than the ones in KL I had visited and I got the impression that it was not so comfortable for the inmates. The young Chinese boy was brought into a room to see me – he could not have been more than about 22 years old – in fact he wasn't when I checked his passport.

He told me that he had been approached in Hong Kong and asked to do this journey – the idea being that he could make enough money to help his family to improve their lives. He said that he had been given all the drugs in Thailand and these had been wrapped around his body in little pouches and also around his arms and legs. I could only imagine what he must have looked like as he waddled over the border – he must have been like the Michelin man or some body building champion – he had drugs secreted all over his body – and not particularly well disguised from what he told me. I strongly suspected that he had been used a sort of decoy. It must have been painfully obvious to anyone who saw him crossing over the border on foot that his body was not normally that shape and that nobody walks like that. I believed and believe to this day that whilst he was walking over the border attracting the attention of all of the Immigration and Customs Officers that a truck load of drugs passed through the border post at the same without being thoroughly examined.

I don't think the boy realised how much trouble he was in because he seemed very relaxed and quite cheerful when I saw him. It must have been his nature, because each time I visited him over the next 12 months or so – he was exactly the same, always happy and smiling. Even after he had been tried and sentenced to death he remained a happy soul who was well liked by his fellow inmates and the prison officers but everyone knew that his day of reckoning would come around eventually. I just hoped that it would not be whilst I was still working at the High Commission. Fortunately – for me – very much aware of what my Australian counterpart had told me previously - I was not. He was still very much alive when I left and I believe lived for a few more years after that. It is almost 15 years ago now so I would imagine his sentence was carried out some time ago and he is already in his grave. What a tragedy – such a nice boy – who believed that he was doing his best to try and help his family.

Chapter 23

On the subject of graves – I received a couple of letters from UK, within a few days of each other. One was from a neighbour of mine in the UK in a little village in Northamptonshire where I had a house, telling me that her brother, who had been in the Army during the second world war had been killed whilst he was fighting the Japanese in Thailand and was buried there. She asked whether it was possible for me to get a picture of his grave because she had never been able to visit Thailand herself and had never even seen pictures of his grave. The other letter was from a lady who was also asking about her brother's grave which was in Malaysia. She said that he had been a British policeman attached to the Malay police force during the communist uprisings in the 1950's. She had also never seen her brother's grave and asked if it was possible for me to go along and take a photograph of it.

The first task, from my neighbour, was relatively easy. I had a friend who I had worked with at the British Embassy in Pretoria who was now working at the British Embassy in Bangkok. She had gone back to London after her tour of duty in South Africa to work in the Foreign Office for a couple of years but had recently been posted to Thailand. I wrote to her, giving her the soldiers details and the location of the grave and asked if she would ask the Consul in Bangkok to take a photograph of it when he next visited the war graves in that particular cemetery. As it turned out it was not the Consul who went to the cemetery but a member of the defence section staff from the Embassy. He very kindly took a couple of photographs of the grave, which Carol, my friend in Bangkok, sent down to me in KL in the diplomatic bag. I forwarded them to my neighbour with a little note to say that I hoped they were alright. She wrote back almost immediately to say that she was extremely grateful. The photographs had arrived on November the 11th – Remembrance Day, which is the day the 1st World War ended. She said that she had always thought about her brother on that day but could not imagine what his grave looked like – having the photographs on that day made her Remembrance Day that year all the more special and more emotional.

The second task was not quite so easy. I had to wait until I was going up to make a prison visit to see the Hong Kong boy in Alor Setar before I could arrange to visit the cemetery which was situated between Ipoh and Penang. I drove up there with some friends from the UK who were visiting Malaysia. We arrived at the cemetery without too much difficulty but finding the grave was not as easy as we thought it was going to be – we had no plan of the cemetery layout and just had to wander about looking for the right headstone. We found the Commonwealth War Grave section of the cemetery easily enough which was in immaculate condition- all the grass was neatly mowed and all the headstones in pristine condition. It looked very smart and very peaceful. When we eventually found the policeman's grave, it was at the far side of the War Graves only a few feet away from where the War Graves section ended. His grave was not in the best of conditions – in fact it was really badly neglected. The grass both on the grave and all around it was long and straggly and the headstone was pretty dirty and covered in moss. Hardly surprising I suppose considering it was not receiving the same amount of care which other graves in that area received from regular visits by friends and relatives bringing flowers. Well we set about trying to clean it up before I took some photographs. We pulled all the long grass up and tried to make the headstone look better by rubbing it to get the moss and dirt off. Unfortunately without the right tools we were unable to get it to look as good as we would have liked to have done. I took some photographs of it, both close up (of the headstone which showed his name) and from a distance so that his sister could see the whole grave. The long distance shot also included a couple of the war graves – which later proved to be a problem.

The lady in the UK wrote to thank me for the photographs but said she was not very happy about her brother's grave being in such a poor condition. She said that she thought that it was disgraceful that her brother's grave was not been taken care of especially when he had given his life fighting with the Malay Police against the communists. She thought that her brother's grave should be looked after by the War Graves Commission seeing as it was only a matter of a couple of feet away from them. Sadly this never happened. I did suggest that she might like to consider employing someone locally who would visit the grave on a regular basis on her behalf and take care of it for her, but I did not hear from her again. Perhaps I should have done what my visiting friend suggested and bought some white chalk to rub all over the headstone before we took the photograph. It would have been a false representation but perhaps his sister would have felt happier. What the eyes don't see the heart won't grieve about.

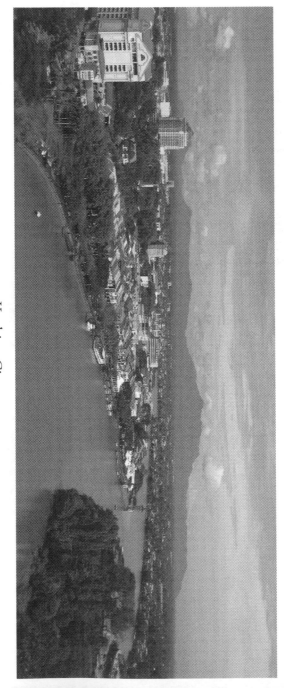

Kuching City

Road to Longhouse

Longhouse

Girls in traditional costume

Girls dancing in traditional costumes

British High Commission Kuala Lumpur

Headhouse in Longhouse

Chapter 24

I was talking to Jane on a regular basis and we both wanted me to go over there more often. I managed to arrange another Consular visit and extended my overnight stay in Miri to 2 nights. I would leave Kuching at the end of the second day and fly up to Kota Kinabalu on the morning of the 4th day. It didn't really matter which city or hotel I stayed overnight as long as I was present at the appointed time in each of the cities I was to visit. The hotel in Miri was actually cheaper than the Hyatt and I was able to organise a nice suite at no extra cost.

I decided, rather than fly over to Kuching on the Sunday as I normally did so as to be ready for the Consular clinic first thing on Monday morning, I would go on the Friday evening so that I could spend the weekend visiting the Longhouse (a communal house on stilts constructed mainly from bamboo) where Jane had been born. I booked a room in the Holiday Inn for the nights of Friday, Sunday and Monday.

After an evening in the Rajang bar catching up with a few friends I was awake bright and early on Saturday morning, excited at what the day had in store for me, and walked down the waterfront in Kuching to the bus station – in the hopes of catching a bus to Annah Rais, which is the name of Jane's longhouse. Annah Rais is situated about 100km to the east of Kuching near the border with Indonesia. I had done some research on Annah Rais and found out that it is an old Bidayuh Tribe Longhouse, with a written history of 175 years and an unwritten history of 500 years, which houses over 80 families. The majority of whom still live in their traditional way of planting paddy, cocoa, pepper, rubber & etc. to eke out a living.

I asked someone who worked at the bus station which bus I should take to get to Annah Rais and he told me that I had just missed it. I asked when the next bus was and he said it would be in the late afternoon. He went on to say that I could catch a bus to a village called Tapah and that it was not far from there to Annah Rais. I asked him how far 'not far' is and he said about 20 minutes. This sounded fine – I didn't mind a 20 minute walk.

Well by the time the bus dropped me off at Tapah, I was already pretty wet and sweaty – the bus was a real old bone shaker with plastic covered seats, no air-conditioning and even with the windows open and the breeze blowing in it was still very hot and humid. The plastic covered seats didn't help either – the back of my shorts and T shirt were saturated with sweat by the time I got off. I crossed the main road and set off at a brisk pace along a much narrower road feeling in good spirits knowing that I was at last going to see a longhouse – not just any old longhouse but the longhouse where Jane had spent her childhood. Well I had been walking for about an hour and could not see any sign of life anywhere let alone the longhouse – the sweat was rolling off of me, the small road seemed to be getting narrower and the jungle seemed to be getting closer and closer to the road. I suddenly remembered what I had read in the newspaper a few weeks earlier about a school girl who had been beheaded as she was walking home from school in Sarawak. Her headless body had been found but there was no trace of her head. It was thought that it had been put into the foundations of a bridge was being built because the locals believe that a skull in the foundations of a bridge makes it much stronger. It seemed that some of the headhunters in that area were still up to their old tricks of decapitating somebody once in a while. I started to whistle to myself to lift my spirits which were getting lower and lower the further I walked. I even started talking to imaginary people in the jungle saying 'anyone in there better be careful because I have a big stick' – not that it would have been much use against anyone using a weapon as silent as a blow pipe with a poison dart - strange what you say to yourself when you are in uncertain situations and surroundings. I had walked for almost two hours when at last I came across a little wooden shack at the side of the road, completely on its own with no other buildings in sight anywhere around, selling ice cold water. Was I hallucinating from de-hydration I wondered. Fortunately not. What a welcome relief. I quenched my thirst and rested for a while before setting off again – all the time cursing the guy at the bus station who told me it was 20 minutes when I suspect what he meant to say was 20 kilometres. After I had walked another couple of miles I heard a van coming from behind me and hope was restored. I immediately stuck my thumb up in the air, turned and put my best smile on (showing all my teeth) in the hope that they would take pity on me and give me a lift. The van was full to bursting and even had people hanging out of the back. As the zoomed past me they all waved and shouted greetings but did not stop, so I kept on walking.

Eventually after about another half an hour or so a motor cyclist pulled up alongside me and offered me a lift – he took me quite a long way but it was still quite a few miles short of Annah Rais. Anyway I was grateful for the lift and also to have some breeze on my face from the speed he was travelling to cool me down. Almost as soon as he had dropped me off another motor cyclist stopped and he took me to within about a mile of Annah Rais – it certainly was at least 20 kilometres from Tapah maybe slightly more - I doubt if I could have walked all that way in the day especially in that heat.

I just had a short, half mile or so, walk along quite a nice road before I came to a small open area in the front of the long house. To the left was a building which I discovered was the library and also the reception area where visitors were asked to sign the visitor's book. The lady in there, Janet Samben, was very helpful and arranged for me to be shown around the long house and also arranged for me to accommodated overnight. I had no idea which was Jane's house but it didn't matter at that moment – I was just pleased and relieved to have arrived. I was taken to one house, which was not part of the longhouse but a three story detached house built along one edge of the longhouses. I was given a room on the top floor and a bamboo mat to sleep on. The toilet and bathroom were on the bottom floor. It was actually very cool in the house and surprisingly enough it seemed much cooler in the longhouse than it did walking along the open road. I suppose it was because of all the trees around and also a fast running stream which dissected the longhouses – the older part being across a bridge at the other side of the stream. Surprisingly enough there were very few mosquitoes - I had half expected to be eaten alive in the longhouse and had come armed with lots of sprays and mosquito coils. My host, a young lady named Jenny, was asking me how I had heard about the Longhouse and when I told her who had mentioned it to me – it turned out that she was one of Jane's cousins. I did not mention Jane and my relationship but I think she must have had some idea. She showed me which was Jane's house and I met Jane's father who was standing outside, and then she took me all over the longhouse including the head hut, where there were skulls hanging in bamboo baskets from the roof – mostly Japanese soldiers so I was told who had been decapitated during the War. I thanked my lucky stars that they appeared to be taking a rest from that activity at the moment.

The longhouse seemed to be a hive of industry – almost everybody seemed to be busy doing something or other – whether it was old ladies, just wearing sarongs with nothing on their sagging boobies, drying rice and weaving baskets out of what appeared to be some kind of grass, or men with long knives hanging from their belts in bamboo scabbards sorting pepper or building new structures out of bamboo. There were also lots of happy children running around the place, playing games and splashing about in the stream, whilst their mother's were busy preparing food. One really pretty little girl, aged about 4 or 5, called Sia Ai Ling, who I suspect by her name and looks was part Chinese, befriended me and was always happy for me to play games with her. Janet sent me a photograph of Sia Ai Ling afterwards wearing the traditional Bidayuh costume - which I still have – she must have changed a lot by now – that was 14 or 15 years ago. She will probably be at University now or already working.

I discovered that there was some special event taking place that night – it was a wedding party - and a lot of the village men were building a temporary structure with lengths of bamboo freshly chopped from the jungle in the part of the longhouse where the party was going to be held. I watched with amazement as the structure started to take shape. Just to make me even more impressed one of the guys, using his machete quickly created a hat peg to hang my hat on and fitted it into a slot he had made in a bamboo upright of the building – fascinating stuff bamboo. There was also a blacksmith in the longhouse making the machetes which all the men seemed to carry. I sat and watched him for ages – working his trade. It reminded me of when I was a blacksmith myself. I even offered to pump his bellows for him but he seemed to be happy and able to manage on his own quite nicely.

As a guest I was given the royal treatment and some locally made rice wine (Tuak) was soon produced and offered around. One of the local guys, who seemed a little bit retarded, decided that he wanted to have a drinking contest with me. Now I am not a big drinker of spirits or any locally made alcohol but I can hold my own when it comes to a few pints of beer. Well after about 4 or 5 large glasses of this stuff, the poor guy was drunk – and had to be taken home – and my reputation as a big drinker was established in the longhouse.

The bride and groom looked splendid in their traditional costumes and there was lots of dancing to the Bidayuh gong music which I was not very good at – having been blessed with two left feet – no wonder I was always last to be selected for a team when it came to playing football in the schoolyard. What an entertaining evening – I was so lucky to have been there that day – it was my first experience of a Bidayuh wedding. The food was really good as well – lots of chicken and rice cooked inside pieces of bamboo by placing the bamboo in the fire. It looked pretty burnt on the outside but the food inside the bamboo was delicious – very tender. Chicken and pork seemed to be their staple diet which explained the number of chickens and pigs which lived underneath the longhouse. They were fed by their owners but also any scraps of food which fell through the bamboo floor of the houses and walkways was quickly gobbled up by either chicken or pigs.

After a long, exhausting day – I was not too late out of bed and slept quite peacefully on the bamboo mat which was my mattress – I suppose the Tuak and some beer helped a lot. It was very quiet in the longhouse and I didn't hear a thing until the cocks started to crow next morning. After breakfast of fried eggs, I decided that I ought to head back into Kuching again to get myself ready for the consular clinic the following morning. Luckily there was a private mini bus, which took people into town for a days shopping and left at about 8.30 am each day so I managed to get a lift on that all the way to the hotel – much better than walking. I was back in the hotel by about 10am to a totally different world from what I had left behind. To be in the longhouse sleeping on the floor on a bamboo mat one night to being in a luxury room in a 5 star hotel the next - what a contrast – but one which I enjoyed and experienced a few more times before I left Malaysia.

Chapter 25

Only 2 more sleeps before I would be in Miri again with Jane. The Consular clinic in Kuching was pretty much the same as it always was, enquiries about student visas, visit visas and passports – no problems at all. On Tuesday afternoon, as soon as I finished my session, I was jumped into a taxi and headed straight to the airport to catch my flight up to Miri.

When I arrived Jane was waiting to meet me at the airport, on her own – which was wonderful, my heart skipped a few beats when I saw her. We managed to make it to her car before kissing and holding each other and it was some time before we actually left the car park to drive into town.

Once we got to the hotel Jane dropped me outside the main entrance and then went to park her car around the other side of the hotel – just in case it was spotted by some of her friends or worse still by her husband if he drove by. I asked if I should wait for her in the lobby but she said that she would catch the service lift up to my floor from the back of the hotel so no-one would see her. All very secretive, but little towns being what they are, it seemed like a good idea to me.

The suite which I had booked was on the top floor of the hotel and had a magnificent view over the town, was wonderful. There was a nice large lounge area with a television and a dining area with an enormous dining room table complete with a basket of fruit and a vase of flowers with a welcome note attached. The bedroom was massive with an en-suite shower room cum toilet – well the shower room was more like a wet room really because it did not have any cubicle as such but just water jets on the wall which sprayed water out and created a very nice almost tropical rain fall effect when switched on. The bed was enormous and it felt very comfortable when I tested it.

Jane arrived, just after I had finished unpacking my small bag and was standing admiring the fruit and flowers. As soon as she came in, we continued where we had left off in the airport car park. I put the do not disturb sign on the door and we made out way to the bedroom – to really test out the king sized bed. She was a little bit shy at first of me seeing her naked – but when we finally removed her clothes she was beautiful from head to toe. We made slow passionate love and then just lay side by side touching each other talking – interspersed with kisses - about what we were going to do in the future. We both felt that we had something really special and should not let it go. Hunger eventually got the better of us in the end so we got out of bed and I rang room service to order some food. As soon as we had eaten we took a shower together, washing each other all over and then it was back to bed again for one last loving session before she had to go home. I don't think I hardly slept that night, thinking about Jane and what had happened to us. Jane told me the next day that she had been the same – a mixture of excitement and wonder of what the future held for us. I felt totally happy – I had never known such happiness. It was the happiest I had been in a long, long time – probably in the whole of my adult life. I never thought love could make me feel like this – but it was a wonderful feeling which gave me a glow inside. The first time in my life I had experienced such a feeling and I couldn't wipe the smile off my face.

The next day at the Consular clinic in Lutong, I was just about floating on air. Nothing seemed to stress me – even the fact that I could not immediately find a taxi to take me there that morning or to bring me back in the evening. The day passed without any problems whatsoever and I headed back to the hotel to get myself ready to meet Jane once again. The plan for that night was slightly different, she would come with Pauline and we would have a drink together in the bar, as we had done previously when Pauline was present so if anyone asked who I was, I could easily be passed off as a friend of Bill's. After dinner we all went up to my room. Pauline, as usual, did not stay very long and left Jane and me together again. It was another wonderful evening of making love and talking about the future. We had both decided that we wanted to be together forever and that the feelings which we had for each other was so special that they should not be allowed to wither and die. I knew when I got back to KL that I was going to speak to my wife and send her back to the UK. I had just been told before I left KL that I had been promoted and was being posted to Malawi in Southern Africa as Management Officer/Consul at the British High Commission in Lilongwe, so we didn't have much time to make arrangements.

Jane left at about 10pm to go home but surprised me next morning by coming to the airport to see me off. We had a few secret kisses and hugs in her car before I left to fly up to Kota Kinabalu to complete the Consular trip. No problems in KK and I was back in Kuala Lumpur on Saturday morning carrying about 100 Malaysian and British passports which were worth about GBP10,000 each on the black market and thousands of Ringgit in my brief case. I was worth about a million and I felt like a million dollars after those two wonderful evenings with Jane.

Within a couple of days of arriving back in Kuala Lumpur I told my wife that I was being posted to Lilongwe in Malawi for 3 years and that I wanted to go there on my own and that I also wanted her to leave Malaysia early. As I imagined she was not very happy about this and we started talking about getting divorced. This suited me fine. She left a day or so later and I was alone at last, happy with my own thoughts of what the future may hold for Jane and me.

Being on my own gave me much more freedom of movement and I made a few weekend visits to Miri because I did not have any Consular visits planned to that part of Malaysia for quite a while. Our love for one another seemed to be getting stronger each time we met – and it was a wrench to leave her each Sunday. We were becoming braver as well – she even drove me passed her house to a small bar just around the corner from where she lived – which much to my surprise played lots of Reba McIntyre songs as well as other Country & Western music – something which I loved. We were as happy as ever – we just had to work out what we were going to do in the future and how we would achieve it.

Chapter 26

Just as I was planning yet another weekend trip over to see Jane, I read in the newspaper that a group of British and Hong Kong soldiers were stranded up Mount Kinabalu in Sabah. It seemed that a group of 7 British soldiers and 3 of their Hong Kong Territorial Army counterparts had been on a training exercise named 'Gully Heights' on Mount Kinabalu, which at 4095.2 metres (13435 ft) is claimed to be the highest mountain between the Himalayas and the mountains of New Guinea. The plan, which I found out later, was that they would march up the tourist trail and then abseil into Low's Gully – a sheer drop of 1.6km onto the virtually unexplored forest floor beneath. On the way down they had become stranded above Low's Gully when they tried to descend down a hitherto different, more hazardous route. I packed my bag immediately and took some temporary passports with me and passport application forms just in case they had lost their belongings whilst up the mountain.

I arrived in KK and checked into the Hyatt hotel so that I would be on hand for any eventuality. The following day I met two of the soldiers who had managed to get down to raise the alarm and they told me that the rest of the group were stranded some way below the summit but could not get back up and could not get down. They had been up there for almost 3 weeks when a group of them, excluding the two officers and the Hong Kong soldiers (one of whom could not walk because he had injured his leg) managed to abseil down 1,800 feet to the gully floor. Once at the bottom they had decided to split up into two groups to give themselves a better chance of raising the alarm. After overcoming fast flowing streams, rapids and thick forest vegetation he and his companion had found the river and followed it downstream. Both of them were starving – their food having run out days earlier. When they finally arrived at Melangkap Tamis village, they met up with the other group and were taken care of by the villagers who provided them with much needed food. They told me it had taken them 5 hours to descend the 1,800 feet to the gully floor in 12 pitches – an amazing achievement. They were both professional soldiers and were somewhat critical about the lack of leadership on the part of their officers, one of whom was a rather unfit reserve list officer on his annual fortnightly training course. They were also critical about the lack of equipment which they had been issued with for the exercise – radios in particular. They said that in their opinion the exercise had been a big mistake. Only one of them was a qualified rock climber and the rest had only had a one day course on abseiling – which was no where near sufficient for a multiple pitch abseil in such hazardous conditions. The guys from Hong Kong were also very unfit and had even struggled walking up the mountain on the tourist trail.

Well we waited and waited for some news about what was happening to the guys who were stranded up the mountain. The hotel started filling up with reporters from all over the world who had arrived to report the story of the stranded British soldiers. A couple of days later I was walking through the hotel lobby one afternoon when I saw this group of extremely fit, lethal looking British young man who were walking around – the sort you don't want to meet in a dark alley. As they were passing me, I overheard one of them say to one of his colleagues – 'Yes Boss' – I realised then who they must be. It could only be a group of British Special Air Service troops who had flown in to assist with the rescue if called upon to do so. I am not sure if any of the local authorities knew they were in town but I felt as though it would not be long before something happened now that the boys in the light blue berets had arrived. As it turned out the rest of the expedition party were eventually rescued by a Malaysian helicopter a day or so later and the boys in the light blue berets disappeared as silently as they had arrived – just like the morning mist.

I grabbed a taxi and went straight to the hospital where the rescued soldiers were being taken to talk to them to see if they required any consular assistance. The journalists were all being kept at bay and were not allowed to enter the hospital but I went in and met with the two officers who had been in charge of the exercise. They seemed to be in a sorry state but after a couple of days had recovered enough to make the journey back to the UK. They had their own version of what had happened up the mountain but I was not in the position to be saying who was right and who was wrong. The Hong Kong soldiers had all lost their bags which contained their passports so I issued them with temporary travel documents so that they could return to Hong Kong. The one with the injured leg confessed to me that he had been scared to death up the mountain – because he was injured and could not walk he imagined that if they had not been rescued he would have died and would have be eaten by his colleagues. I think he must have been watching that movie about the South American rugby team whose plane crashed in the Andes and the survivors ate the bodies of those who had died – just to stay alive.

As I came out of the hospital one day, an Australian journalist came up to me and said "who the hell are you? We have seen you in the hotel this last few days talking to people who we never get the chance to speak to and you swan in and out of the hospital here whilst we are kept waiting outside". Perhaps a little bit mischievously – I said I'm afraid I can't tell you that. That really got them wondering.

Chapter 27

One of my last Consular tasks before I left Kuala Lumpur was to go to court with a group of British Rugby players from a well know London Rugby club. They had been in KL to play in a 7 a-side rugby tournament. After one of their final games a group of them decided to stand on the touchline and bare their backsides to one of the New Zealand Rugby teams who were playing at that particular time – not realising that some quick shooting photographer would take a shot of them with their shorts down and their backsides bare. Well next day it was splashed across the front page of the Kuala Lumpur newspaper with an article which described them as being very rude for making such offensive gestures during the rugby tournament. They were told that they had to appear in court the following day for indecent exposure, so I had to go along to see what was going to happen to them, especially as they already had their flights booked for that evening. It was a lady judge who presided over their hearing and she seemed to spend quite a long time looking at the photographs – so much so that one of the rugby players had lots of 'off the cuff' comments to make about her once she had announced sentence – of a small fine. I won't mention what the black rugby player had to say but it was something to do with the judge being fascinated by the size of a certain part of his anatomy.

Chapter 28

Time was getting short now and I was only a matter of weeks away from ending my tour of duty in Malaysia. I managed to arrange a few days off and went over to Kuching to meet Jane, who had also arranged a few days off and was going to fly down from Miri to Kuching. The plan was that we would meet at the airport and then go down to the Holiday Inn Damai Beach resort – about half an hours drive outside of Kuching on the coast of the South China Sea.

I arrived a day early so that I could go out to the longhouse first to say a final farewell to all my friends out there – especially little Sia Ai Ling. The next morning I caught the mini shopping bus along with a group other people from the Longhouse who were going into Kuching. Not long after we had left the longhouse the young lady who was sitting next to me started putting her hand on my knee each time the bus went over some rough ground. It seemed to be rough ground all the way into Kuching because her hand was on my knee for most of the way. When we arrived in town we dropped her off at her hotel and she asked me to give her a ring if I wanted to go out that evening. Not me – I was waiting for Jane. When I got to my hotel there was a message waiting for me from Jane saying that she could not make it that day and would try and get down the next day. What a disappointment. After sitting in my room in the hotel for a while wondering what I should do, I received a phone call from the girl on the bus asking what I was doing that evening. When I replied that I had nothing planned she suggested we have dinner together in a restaurant near her hotel – no harm in that I thought - so fool that I was I agreed.

Well once I arrived at the hotel I phoned her room to say I was waiting downstairs for her in the lobby. She said she wasn't quite ready yet and asked me to go up to her room. When I got there she was just finishing off putting her make up on and just as we were about to leave the heavens opened and it started raining cats and dogs. The rain was coming down, as it does in Malaysia, like stair rods. We were stuck for an hour or so at least till it stopped. She lay on the bed and suggested I lay down with her – well one thing led to another and I did the most stupid thing I could possibly have done – I had sex with her.

I was disgusted with myself afterwards and more to the point I was worried sick about what Jane would have to say if she ever found out – especially as this girl was one of Jane's cousins. Well Jane did find out – courtesy of her cousin who could not wait to tell her. I was in big trouble – and did not see Jane during that visit to Kuching.

It took many helpings of humble pie before Jane finally forgave me and our relationship resumed where we had left off so I went over to Miri for the last time. When it finally came time for me to return to KL to get ready to leave for good – we had made plans that I would send for her once I arrived in Malawi. I had some courses to do in London first in the Foreign Office so it would be a couple of months before I would be able to send for her. Everything seemed to be agreed, and I was looking forward to life with Jane.

Chapter 29

My tour of duty was almost up at the High Commission in KL. With just 3 days to go before I left, I moved out of my house to the Crown Princess Hotel, which is a very nice hotel just across the road from the High Commission. My house needed to be painted and decorated etc ready for my replacement to move into when he arrived.

The second evening there, as I was returning from my usual hours jog in a near by park, I was walking through the lobby to the lift when who should appear from behind one of the pillars but Jane. What a wonderful surprised. I couldn't believe my eyes I was absolutely delighted to see her – she looked absolutely gorgeous. I thought she had just flown over from East Malaysia so that she could spend the last night with me and see me off at the airport the following day.

Well when we got up to my room she told me that she had left her husband and that she had taken GBP3,000 out of their joint savings account to buy clothes etc – some of which she was wearing – and was coming with me to London the following day when I left. As pleased as I was to hear this I had to explain that it simply was not possible. I still had to get divorced, and if she came with me I had to find a place for us both to live, on top of which I had to go away on the different residential courses which had already been arranged for me by the Foreign Office.

Needless to say she was heartbroken and no matter what I said nothing seemed to console her. I really wanted to be with her but the timing had to be right.

She left the following day to return to her home in Miri to face the wrath of her husband who she was sure would be absolutely furious with her. I didn't know what to do or say. I tried to reassure her that I would definitely send for her once I got to Malawi but she did not seem to believe me anymore. She was heartbroken – I had never seen her cry before and it was awful. I felt guilty as sin - as though I had failed her and let her down completely – especially when she told me she had never cried over a man before in her whole life.

She never did come to join me in Malawi but I saw her again about 4 years later when I stopped off in East Malaysia enroute to China to take up a new posting with the FCO as Her Majesty's Consul at the British Embassy in Beijing. I flew up to Miri and met her with Pauline and asked if she would consider coming to join me in Beijing. As soon as I saw her I knew that the feelings I had for her were still as strong as ever – she said she felt the same way, but whilst 80 per cent of her wanted to come with me there was 20 per cent of her which didn't trust me any more. This time it was me who was heartbroken.

I left with a heavy heart and tears in my eyes – just like the Royal Selangor Pewter elephant I had given to Jane as a present before I left her 4 years earlier. I left East Malaysia the following day and flew up to Beijing to start a new job in China where one of my first Consular cases, within a matter of a couple of weeks of arriving, was the murder of a British Citizen – but that is another story for another time.